Problems of the

Frank Fox

Alpha Editions

This edition published in 2024

ISBN 9789362511614

Design and Setting By
Alpha Editions
www.alphaedis.com
Email - info@alphaedis.com

As per information held with us this book is in Public Domain.
This book is a reproduction of an important historical work.
Alpha Editions uses the best technology to reproduce historical work
in the same manner it was first published to preserve its original nature.
Any marks or number seen are left intentionally to preserve.

Contents

CHAPTER I	- 1 -
CHAPTER II	- 9 -
CHAPTER III	- 17 -
CHAPTER IV	- 25 -
CHAPTER V	- 35 -
CHAPTER VI	- 45 -
CHAPTER VII	- 53 -
CHAPTER VIII	- 64 -
CHAPTER IX	- 72 -
CHAPTER X	- 78 -
CHAPTER XI	- 87 -
CHAPTER XII	- 92 -
CHAPTER XIII	- 98 -
CHAPTER XIV	- 105 -
CHAPTER XV	- 114 -
CHAPTER XVI	- 120 -
CHAPTER XVII	- 128 -
CHAPTER XVIII	- 137 -

CHAPTER I

THE OCEAN OF THE FUTURE

The Pacific is the ocean of the future. As civilisation grows and distances dwindle, man demands a larger and yet larger stage for the fighting-out of the ambitions of races. The Mediterranean sufficed for the settlement of the issues between the Turks and the Christians, between the Romans and the Carthaginians, between the Greeks and the Persians, and who knows what other remote and unrecorded struggles of the older peoples of its littoral. Then the world became too great to be kept in by the Pillars of Hercules, and Fleets—in the service alike of peace and war—ranged over the Atlantic. The Mediterranean lost its paramount importance, and dominance of the Atlantic became the test of world supremacy.

Now greater issues and greater peoples demand an even greater stage. On the bosom of the Pacific will be decided, in peace or in war, the next great struggle of civilisation, which will give as its prize the supremacy of the world. Shall it go to the White Race or the Yellow Race? If to the White Race, will it be under the British Flag, or the flag of the United States, or of some other nation? That is the problem of the Pacific.

Since Cortes first looked on the waters of the ocean from a peak in Darien, since Balboa of Castile waded into its waters and claimed them for the dominion of the King of Castile, events have rushed forward with bewildering haste to transfer the centre of the world's interest to the Pacific. Cortes in his day looked to a North Pacific coast inhabited by a few wandering Indians. (The powerful national organisation of Mexico had not extended its influence as far as the Pacific coast.) Now there stretch along that coast the Latin-American Power of Mexico, doomed, probably, to be absorbed before the great issue of Pacific dominance is decided, but having proved under Diaz some capacity for organisation; the gigantic Power of the United States with the greatest resources of wealth and material force ever possessed by a single nation of the world; and the sturdy young Power of Canada.

To the South, Cortes looked to a collection of Indian States, of which Peru was the chief, boasting a gracious but unwarlike civilisation, doomed to utter destruction at the hands of Spain. Now that stretch of Pacific littoral is held by a group of Latin-American nations, the possibilities of which it is difficult accurately to forecast, but which are in some measure formidable if

Chili is accepted as a standard by which to judge, though, on the whole, they have shown so far but little capacity for effective national organisation.

Looking westward, Cortes in his day could see nothing but darkness. It was surmised rather than known that there lay the Indies, the kingdoms of the Cham of Tartary and the great Mogul, lands which showed on the horizon of the imagination, half real, half like the fantasy of a mirage. To-day the west coast of the Pacific is held by the European Power of Russia; by the aspiring Asiatic Power of Japan, which within half a century has forgotten the use of the bow and the fan in warfare and hammered its way with modern weapons into the circle of the world's great Powers; by China, stirring uneasily and grasping at the same weapons which won greatness for Japan; by a far-flung advance guard of the great Power of the United States in the Philippines, won accidentally, held grimly; by England's lonely outposts, Australia and New Zealand, where less than five millions of the British race hold a territory almost as large as Europe.

Sprinkled over the surface of the ocean, between East and West, are various fortresses or trading stations, defending interests or arousing cupidities. Germany and France are represented. The United States holds Hawaii, the key to the Pacific coast of North America, either for offence or defence. Great Britain has Fiji and various islets. The Japanese Power stretches down towards the Philippines with the recent acquisition of Formosa.

Here are seen all the great actors in European rivalry. Added to them are the new actors in world-politics, who represent the antagonism of the Yellow Race to the White Race. Before all is dangled the greatest temptation to ambition and cupidity. Who is master of the Pacific, who has the control of its trade, the industrial leadership of its peoples, the disposal of its warrior forces, will be master of the world.

It is a problem not only of navies and armies (though with our present defective civilisation these are the most important factors): it is a problem also of populations and their growth, of industries, of the development of natural resources, of trade and commerce. The Pacific littoral is in part unpeopled, in part undeveloped, unorganised, unappropriated. Its Asiatic portion must change, it is changing, from a position which may be compared with that of Japan fifty years ago to a position such as Japan's to-day. Its American and Australian portion must develop power and wealth surpassing that of Europe. Under whose leadership will the change be made? To discuss that question is the purpose of this book: and at the outset the lines on which the discussion will proceed and the conclusions which seem to be inevitable may be foreshadowed.

At one time Russia seemed destined to the hegemony of the Pacific. Yet she was brought to the Pacific coast by accident rather than by design. Her natural destiny was westward and southward rather than eastward, though it was natural that she should slowly permeate the Siberian region. As far back as the reign of Ivan the Terrible (the Elizabethan epoch in Anglo-Saxon history), the curious celibate military organisation of the Cossacks had won much of Siberia for the Czars. But there was no dream then, nor at a very much later period, of penetration to the Pacific.

European jealousy of Russia, a jealousy which is explainable only with the reflection that vast size naturally fills with awe the human mind, stopped her advance towards the Mediterranean. In the north her ports were useless in winter. In the south she was refused a development of her territory which was to her mind natural and just. Thus thwarted, Russia groped in a blind way from the Siberian provinces which had been won by the Cossacks towards a warm-water port in Asia. At first the movement was southward and filled England with alarm as to the fate of India. Then it turned eastward, and in Manchuria and Corea this European Power seemed to find its destiny. But Japan was able to impose an effective check upon Russian ambitions in the Far East. At the present moment Russia has been supplanted in control of the Asiatic seaboard by Japan.

Japan has everything but money to equip her for a bold bid for the mastery of the Pacific before the completion of the Panama Canal. Europe has taught to Japan, in addition to the material arts of warfare, a cynical faith in the moral value, indeed, the necessity, of war to national welfare. She considers that respect is only to be gained by war: that war with a European nation is an enterprise of small risk: that in short her experience with the Russian Fleet was fairly typical of war with any European Power. She believes that she has the most thoroughly efficient army and navy, considering their size, in the world; and has much to justify the belief.

This ambition and the warlike confidence of Japan constitute to-day a more important factor in the problem of the Pacific than her actual fighting strength. But the check to prompt decisive action on her part is that of poverty. Japan is very poor. The last war, in spite of great gain of prestige, brought no gain of money. Its cost bled her veins white, and there was no subsequent transfusion in the shape of a Russian indemnity. Nor are the natural resources of Japan such as to hold out much hope of a quick industrial prosperity. She has few minerals. Her soil is in the bulk wretchedly poor. From the territories control of which she has won in battle—Manchuria and Corea—she will reap some advantage by steadily ignoring the "open door" obligation in trade, and by dispossessing the native peasantry. But it cannot be very great. There is no vast natural wealth to be exploited. The native peasantry can be despoiled and evicted, but the booty is trifling and the cost of the process not inconsiderable since even the Corean will shoot from his last ditch.

Japan is now seeking desperately a material prosperity by industrial expansion. A tariff and bounty system, the most rigid and scientific the world knows, aims to make the country a great textile-weaving, ship-building, iron-making country. The smallest scrap of an industry is sedulously nurtured, and Japanese matches, Japanese soap, Japanese beer, penetrate to the markets of the outer world as evidence of the ambition of the people to be manufacturers. But when one explores down to bedrock, the only real bases for industrial prosperity in Japan are a supply of rather poor coal and a great volume of cheap labour. The second is of some value in cheap production, but it is yet to be found possible to build up national prosperity on the sole basis of cheap labour. Further, with the growth of modernity in Japan, there is naturally a labour movement. Doctrines of Socialism are finding followers: strikes are heard of occasionally. The Japanese artisan and coolie may not be content to slave unceasingly on wages which deny life all comfort, to help a method of national aggrandisement the purport of which they can hardly understand.

The position of Japan in the Pacific has to be considered, therefore, in the light of the future rather than of the present. At the time of the conclusion of the war with Russia it seemed supreme. Since then it has steadily deteriorated. If she had succeeded in the realisation of her ambition to undertake the direction of China's military and industrial reorganisation, the Japanese Power would have been firmly established for some generations at least. But the defects in her national character prevented that. Inspiring no confidence among the Chinese, the Japanese found all attempts at peaceful assumption of a controlling influence in China checked by sullen antipathy; and a forced assumption would not have been tolerated by Europe. It will not be found possible, on a full survey of the facts, to credit Japan with the power to hold a supreme place in the Pacific. She is, even now, among the dwindling Powers.

China, on the other hand, has the possibilities of a mighty future. To-day she is in the throes of nation-birth. To-morrow she may unbind her feet and prepare to join in the race for supremacy. The bringing of China into the current of modern life will not be an easy task, but it is clearly not an impossible one. Before the outbreak of the present Revolution (which may place China among the democratic Republics of the world), the people of the Celestial Empire had begun to reconsider seriously their old attitude of intolerance towards European civilisation. To understand fully the position of China it is necessary to keep in mind the fact that the actual Chinese nation, some 400,000,000 of people, enervated as were the Peruvians of South America, by a system of theocratic and pacific Socialism, were subjected about 250 years ago to the sovereignty of the Manchus, a warrior race from the Steppes. Since then the Manchus have governed China, tyrannously, incompetently, on the strength of a tradition of military superiority stronger far than the *Raj* by which the British have held India. But the Manchus—in numbers and in intellect far inferior to the Chinese—forgot in time their military enterprise and skill. The tradition of it, however, remained until the events of the nineteenth and twentieth centuries showed that the Manchu military power was contemptible not only against the white foreigner, but also against the Japanese *parvenu*. Patient China, finding her tyrant to be a weak despot, revolts now, not only against the Manchu dynasty, but also against the Conservatism which has kept her from emulating Japan's success in the world.

At present the power of China in the Pacific is negligible. In the future it may be the greatest single force in that ocean. Almost certainly it may be reckoned to take the place of Japan as the chief Asiatic factor.

Japan and China having been considered, the rest of Asia is negligible as affecting the destiny of the Pacific except in so far as India can serve as basis of action for British power. An independent Indian nation is hardly one of the possibilities of the future. Religious, racial, and caste distinctions make a united, independent India at present impossible. Unless the British Power carries too far a tendency to conciliate the talking tribes of the Hindoo peninsula at the expense of the fighting tribes, it should hold India by right of a system of government which is good though not perfect, and by reason of the impossibility of suggesting any substitute. In the event of a failure of the British Power, India would still, in all probability, fail to take a place among the great nations of the earth. Either she would fall a victim to some other nation or relapse into the condition, near to anarchy, which was hers before the coming of the Europeans.

It is not possible to imagine to-day any European Power other than Great Britain—with the possible exception of Russia—becoming strongly established in the Pacific. France and Germany have footholds certainly. But in neither case is the territory held by them possible of great development, and in neither case is there a chain of strategic stations to connect the Pacific colony with the Mother Country. The despatch of the German "mailed fist" to Kiao-Chou in China some years ago is still remembered as one of the comic rather than the serious episodes of history. The squadron bearing to the Chinese the martial threat of the German Emperor had to beg its way from one British coaling station to another because of the lack of German ports.

The influence of South America in the Pacific need not yet be calculated. It is a possible far-future factor in the problem; and the completion of Trans-Andine railways may quickly enhance the importance of Chili and Peru. But for the present South America can take no great part in the Pacific struggle.

It is when British influence and American influence in the Pacific come to be considered that the most important factors in the contest for its supremacy enter upon the stage. Let us consider, for the nonce, the two Powers separately.

The British Empire—holding Australia and New Zealand with an audacious but thin garrison; having a long chain of strategic stations such as Hong Kong and Singapore; having in India a powerful rear base for supplies; holding a great part of the North-West Coast of America with a population as yet scanty but beginning to develop on the same lines as the Australasian people—is clearly well situated to win and to hold the mastery of the Pacific. Such mastery would have to be inspired with peaceful ideals; it could not survive as an aggressive force. It is indeed the main strength of the British position in the Pacific that it is naturally anxious, not for a disturbance but for a preservation of the present state of things, which gives to the British Empire all that a reasonable ambition could require. It is wise and easy to be peaceable when one has all the best of the spoils.

For a secure British mastery of the Pacific, India would need to be held with the military assistance of South Africa and Australia, and made a great naval base; Australia and New Zealand would need to be populated seriously; Canada would need to be guarded against absorption by the United States and its new population kept as far as possible to the British type; the friendship and co-operation of the United States would need to be sought.

Turning next to the United States it will be recognised that she has in a realised form all the force and wealth possible to an organised China or a fully developed Australia. She has one hundred million people, who have reached the highest stage of civilised organisation. Their material wealth—and wealth counts for much in modern war—is almost incalculable. Their national ambition has never been checked by defeat. Lately it has been fed with foreign war and territorial conquest and it has found the taste good. The American people face the future possessed of all the material for a policy of aggressive Imperialism and with a splendidly youthful faith in their own good motives, a faith which can justify an action better than any degree of cynicism. There is as much of the "old Adam" in them as in the peoples of any of the "effete monarchies," and many circumstances seem to point to them as anxious to take the lead among the White Races in the future.

As regards the Pacific, American ambition is clear. The United States holds the Philippines at great expense of treasure and blood. She is fortifying Honolulu, with the idea of making it a naval base "stronger than Gibraltar." [1] She is cutting the Panama Canal and fortifying the entrances with the probable purpose of giving to the United States a monopoly of that gateway in time of war. With splendid audacity the American despises secrecy in regard to his future plans. In New York Naval Yard three years ago I was informed, with an amplitude of detail that was convincing, of the United States' scheme for patrolling the whole Pacific with her warships when the Canal had been finished.

Supposing, then, the United States to continue her present industrial and commercial progress; supposing her to gradually tighten her hold on the rest of the American continent; supposing her to overcome certain centrifugal forces now at work, the problem of the Pacific, should the United States decide to play a "lone hand," will be solved. It will become an American lake, probably after a terrible struggle in which the pretensions of the Yellow Races will be shattered, possibly after another fratricidal struggle in which the British possessions in the Pacific, Australia, and New Zealand, equally with Canada, will be forced to obedience.

But is there any necessity to consider the United States and the British Empire as playing mutually hostile parts in the Pacific? They have been the best of friends there in the past. They have many good reasons to remain friends in the future. A discussion as to whether the Pacific Ocean is destined to be controlled by the American or by the British Power could be reasonably ended with the query: Why not by an Anglo-Celtic union representing both?

An Anglo-Celtic alliance embracing Great Britain, the United States and the British Dominions, would settle in the best way the problem of the Pacific. No possible combination, Asiatic, European, or Asia-European, could threaten its position. But there are certain difficulties in the way, which will be discussed later. For the present, it has only to be insisted that both Powers are potential rather than actual masters of the Pacific. Neither in the case of Great Britain nor of the United States is a great Pacific force at the moment established. After her treaty with Japan, Great Britain abandoned for a while the idea of maintaining any serious naval strength in the Pacific. The warships she maintained there, on the Australian station and elsewhere, had no fighting value against modern armaments, and were kept in the Pacific as a step towards the scrap-heap. That policy has since been reversed, and the joint efforts of Great Britain, Australia, and New

Zealand directed towards re-establishing British Pacific naval strength. At the moment, however, the actual British naval force in the Pacific is inconsiderable, if obsolete or obsolescent vessels are ruled out of consideration. The United States also has no present naval force in the Pacific that could contest the issue with even a fraction of the Japanese navy. Clearly, too, she has no intention of attempting the organisation of a powerful Pacific Fleet separate from her Atlantic Fleet, but aims at the bolder policy of holding her interests in both oceans by one great Fleet which will use the Panama Canal to mobilise at an emergency in either.

If the resources of the present with their probable growth in the future are taken into account, Great Britain and the United States will appear as massing enormous naval and military forces in the Pacific. The preponderance of naval force will be probably on the side of the United States for very many years—since it is improbable that Great Britain will ever be able to detach any great proportion of her Fleet from European waters and her Pacific naval force will be comprised mainly of levies from Australia and New Zealand, and possibly Canada, India, and South Africa. The preponderance of military force will be probably on the side of Great Britain, taking into count the citizen armies of Australia and New Zealand (and possibly of Canada) and the great forces available in India. Complete harmony between Great Britain and the United States in the Pacific would thus give the hegemony of the ocean to the Anglo-Saxon race. Rivalry between them might lead to another result. In the natural course of events that "other result" might be Asiatic dominion in one form or another.

These factors in Pacific rivalry will be discussed in detail in the following chapters.

CHAPTER II

RUSSIA IN THE PACIFIC

Russia, for generations the victim of Asia, when at last she had won to national greatness, was impelled by pressure from the West rather than by a sense of requital to turn back the tide of invasion. That pressure from the West was due to a misunderstanding in which Great Britain led the way, and which the late Lord Salisbury happily described when he stated that England "had backed the wrong horse" in opposing Russia and in aiding Turkey against her.

Russia, because she broke Napoleon's career of victory by her power of resistance, a power which was founded on a formlessness of national life rather than a great military strength, was credited by Europe with a fabulous might. Properly understood, the successful Russian resistance to the greatest of modern captains was akin to that of an earthwork which absorbs the sharpest blows of artillery and remains unmoved, almost unharmed. But it was misinterpreted, and a mental conception formed of the Russian earthwork as a mobile, aggressive force eager to move forward and to overwhelm Europe. Russia's feat of beating back the tide of Napoleonic invasion was merely the triumph of a low biological type of national organism. Yet it inspired Europe with a mighty fear. The "Colossus of the North" came into being to haunt every Chancellery.

Nowhere was the fear felt more acutely than in Great Britain. It is a necessary consequence of the British Imperial expansion of the past, an expansion that came about very often in spite of the Mother Country's reluctance and even hostility, that Great Britain must now always view with distrust, with suspicion, that country which is the greatest of the European Continental Powers for the time being, whether it be France, Russia, or Germany. If British foreign policy is examined carefully it will be found to have been based on that guiding principle for many generations. Whatever nation appears to aim at a supreme position in Europe must be confronted by Great Britain.

Sometimes British statesmen, following instinctively a course which was set for them by force of circumstances, have not recognised the real reason of their actions. They have imagined that there was some ethical warrant for the desire for a European "balance of power." They have seen in the malignant disposition of whatever nation was the greatest Power in Europe for the time being a just prompting to arrange restraining coalitions, to wage crippling wars. But the truth is that the British race, with so much that is desirable of the earth under its flag, with indeed almost all the good empty lands in its keeping, must be jealous of the next European Power. On the other hand, every growing Power in Europe must look with envy on the rich claim which one prospector, and that one not the earliest, has pegged out in the open fields of the world. Thus between Great Britain and the next European Power in rank there is always a mutual jealousy. The growing Power is credited with a desire to seize the rich lands of the British Empire; and generally has the desire. The holding Power is apprehensive of every step forward of any rival, seeing in it a threat to her Empire's security. There is such a thing in this world as being too rich to be comfortable. That is Great Britain's national position.

Thus when the power of France was broken and Napoleon was safely shut up in St Helena, the British nation, relieved of one dread, promptly found another. Russia was credited with designs on India. She was supposed to be moving south towards the Mediterranean, and her object in seeking to be established there was obviously to challenge British naval supremacy, and to capture British overseas colonies. British diplomacy devoted itself sternly to the task of checkmating Russia. Russia, the big blundering amorphous nation, to whom England had given, some generations before, early promptings to national organisation, and who now sprawled clumsily across Europe groping for a way out of her ice-chains towards a warm-water port, became the traditional enemy of the British Empire.

This idea of Russian rivalry grew to be an obsession. The melodramas of the British people had for their favourite topic the odious cruelty of Russian tyranny. If a submarine cable to a British colony were interrupted, or a quarry explosion startled the air, the colonists at once turned their thoughts to a Russian invasion, and mobilised their volunteers. Colonists of this generation can remember the thrills of early childhood, when more than once they "prepared for the Russians," and the whole force of some hundreds of volunteers and cadets determined to sell their lives dearly on the battlefield to keep Russian knouts from the backs of their womenfolk, it being seriously considered that the Russian always celebrated a victory by a general knouting.

Not until the idea of Russia establishing a hegemony over Europe had been dissipated by the Russo-Japanese War did British statesmanship really discover qualities of good neighbourliness in the Russian. But by that time the main direction of Russian expansion had been definitely settled as eastward instead of southward. Perhaps this was to the ultimate advantage of civilisation, even though the decision left the Hellenic peninsula in the grip of the Turk, for it pushed the buffer territory between Europe and Asia far forward into Asia. Should an Asiatic Power, with revived militancy, ever seek again the conquest of Europe, as Asiatic Powers have done before this, the war must commence in Manchuria, and not on the plains below the Ural Mountains.

The position which Russia has occupied as a buffer state between Asia and Europe has kept her back in the ranks of the army of civilisation. Not only has she had to suffer the first of the savage blows which Asian hordes have from time to time aimed at Europe, but also she has had to endure Asiatic additions to her population, reducing the standard of her race.

The instinct against race-mixture which Nature has implanted in man is the great safeguard of the work of evolution to a higher type. The White Race, having developed on certain lines to a position which promises, if it does not fulfil, the evolution of a yet higher type, has an instinctive repugnance to mixing its blood with peoples in other stages of evolution. It is this instinct, this transcendental instinct, which is responsible for the objection to miscegenation in the United States, and for the lynchings by which that objection is impressed upon the negro mind. The same instinct is at the back of the "White Australia" laws, forbidding coloured people any right of entry into Australia.

It is not difficult to argue from a point of view of Christian religion and humanity against an instinct which finds its extreme, but yet its logical, expression in the burning of some negro offender at the stake. But all the arguments in the world will not prevail against Nature. Once a type has won a step up it must be jealous and "selfish," and even brutal in its scorn of lower types; or must climb down again. This may not be good ethics, but it is Nature. Russian backwardness in civilisation to-day is a living proof that the scorn of the coloured man is a necessary condition of the progress of the White Man's civilisation.

But the race-mixture which was of evil to Russia has been of benefit to the rest of Europe. To borrow a metaphor from modern preventive medicine, the Russian marches between Europe and Asia have had their power of resistance to Yellow invasion strengthened by the infusion of some Yellow blood.

A land of high steppes, very cold in winter, very hot in summer, and of great forests, which were difficult to traverse except where the rivers had cut highways, Russia was never so tempting to the early European civilisations as to lead to her area being definitely occupied and held as a province. Neither Greek nor Roman attempted much colonisation in Russia. By general consent the country was left to be a No-Man's-Land between Asia and Europe. Alexander, whose army penetrated through to India and actually brought back news of the existence of Australia, never marched far north into the interior of Russia. There the mixed tribes of Finns, Aryans, Semites, Mongols held a great gloomy country influenced little by civilisation, but often temporarily submerged by waves of barbarians from the Asiatic steppes. Still Western Europe in time made some little impression on the Russian mass. Byzantine culture impressed its mark on the Southern Slavs; Roman culture, after filtering through Germany, reached the Lithuanians of the north. In the twelfth century we hear of Arabian caravans making their way as far as the Baltic in search of amber.

But more important to the Russian civilisation was the advent of the Normans in the ninth century. They consolidated White Russia during the ninth to the thirteenth centuries, appeared as warriors before the walls of Byzantium, and learned the Christian faith from the priests of the Eastern communion. (Russia has since been faithful always to the Greek Church.) That period was rich in national heroes, such as Rurik, Simeon and Truvor, and definitely set the current of Russian national life towards a place in the European family of nations. By the thirteenth century the White Russians, with their capital established at Moscow, were able to withstand for a while a new Mongol invasion. But they could not prevent Gengis Khan's lieutenants establishing themselves on the lower Volga, and the Grand Prince of Moscow had to be content to become a suzerain of the Grand Khan of Tartary.

For three centuries Russia now, amid many troubles, prepared herself to take a place amongst European Powers. She was still more or less subject to the Asiatic. But she was not Asiatic, and her vast area stood between Europe and Asia and allowed the more Western nations to grow up free from interference from any Eastern people, except in the case of the great invasion of the Turks coming up from the south-east. How great was the service that Russia unconsciously did to civilisation during those centuries! If the Tartar had come with the Turk, or had followed him, the White Races and their civilisation might have been swept away.

After being the bulwark of Europe for centuries Russia at last found her strength and became the avenger of the White Races. By the sixteenth century the Russian power had been consolidated under the Muscovite Czars, and a great nation, of which the governing class was altogether European, began to push back the Asiatic. From the sixteenth to the nineteenth centuries the Russian Power grew. The natural direction of expansion was southward. The new nation wanted a place in the sun, and looked longingly towards the Mediterranean. Only the Turk stood in the path, and for the Russian Czars war with the Turk had something of a religious attraction. It was the Cross against the Crescent. It was the champion of the Greek Church winning back the Byzantine Empire to Christian domination.

For Russia to march south, driving the infidel from Europe, freeing the Greeks, establishing herself in Constantinople, winning warm-water ports and warm-climate fields, seemed to the Russian mind a national policy which served both God and Mammon. That it served God was no slight thing to the Russian people. They, then as now, cherished a simplicity and a strenuousness of faith which may be called "superstitious" or "beautiful and childlike" as the observer may wish, but which is undoubtedly sincere. "There has been only one Christian," wrote Heine. If he had known the Russians he would have qualified the gibe. They have a real faith, and it is an important factor in the making of their national policy which has to be taken into account.

How much there was of religious impulse and how much of mere materialistic national ambition in Russia's move southward did not in the least concern other European Powers. Whatever its motive they considered the development dangerous. It threatened to give the Russian an overwhelming power, a paramountcy in Europe, and that could not be tolerated even if it had the most worthy of motives. Above all, Great Britain was alarmed. In the days of Elizabeth Great Britain had been a very good friend to Russia. But Russia was then no possible rival either on land or on the high seas. In the days of Victoria the position had changed. Russia still wore the laurels of her "victories" over Napoleon. She was credited with being the greatest military Power in the world, and credited also with a relentless and Machiavellian diplomacy that added vastly to the material resources of her armies and fleets.

The Crimean War, with its resulting humiliating restrictions on Russian power in the Black Sea, taught Russia that Europe was determined to block her path south and preferred to buttress Turkish misrule than to permit Russian expansion. Baffled but still restless, Russia turned east and marched steadily towards the Pacific, with a side glance at the Persian Gulf and the Indian Ocean, which caused Great Britain fresh apprehension as to the fate of India.

The progress of the Russian Power in Asia throughout the nineteenth century and its sudden check at the dawn of the twentieth century make one of the most dramatic chapters of the world's history. European rivalry had followed Russia on her march across Siberia, and the British Power in particular was alarmed to see the "Colossus of the North" with a naval base in the Pacific. Alarm was deepened when, after reaching the waters of the Pacific, Russia turned south, again eager for a warm-water port. At the time China seemed to be on the verge of dissolution as a national entity, and it seemed as though Russia were destined to win a great Asiatic Empire beside which even India would be a poor prize. In 1885 Great Britain nearly went to war with Russia in the defence of the integrity of Corea.

But the decisive check to Russia was to come from another source. The time had arrived for Asia to reassert some of her old warlike might. The island power of Japan, having shaken off the cumbrous and useless armour of medievalism, set herself sturdily in the path of modern progress and aspired to a place among the great nations of the earth. Japan saw clearly that Russia was the immediate enemy and prepared for a decisive war, with an uncanny determinedness and a scrupulous attention to every detail. Vast military and naval armaments had to be prepared. The necessary money had to be wrung from a bitterly poor population or borrowed at usurious rates. The political art with which that was done was not the least wonderful part of a great national achievement. Then—the weapons of war forged—it seemed good to Japanese statesmanship to flesh them on an easy victim. It fell to China's lot to teach the Japanese confidence in their new warlike arts, and to pay in the shape of an indemnity something towards the cost of the great struggle which Japan contemplated.

Had Russia had that relentless and Machiavellian diplomacy with which she used to be credited, she would never have permitted the Japanese attack upon China. Constituting herself the champion of China, she would at one stroke have pushed back the growing power of Japan and established a claim to some suzerainty over the Celestial Empire. In carrying out her plans Japan had to take this chance, of Russia coming on top of her when she attacked China. She took the chance and won. Russia would have had to take the chance of a great European upheaval if she had interfered in the Japo-Chinese struggle. She did not take the chance, and allowed her rival to arm at China's expense to meet her.

The Chinese war finished, Japan, equipped with a full war-chest, a veteran army and navy, was now ready to meet Russia. But she was faced by the difficulty that in meeting Russia she might also have to meet a European coalition, or the almost equally dangerous eventuality of a veto on the war on the part of the United States. Japan was convinced of her ability to fight Russia single-handed. Probably she would, in the last event, have decided to take the risks of any coalition and enter upon the war, since she had to fight Russia or perish as an expanding Power. But she determined in the first instance to attempt to obtain a safeguarding alliance.

There are indications that Japan had in the first instance thoughts of the United States, of Germany and of Great Britain, as alternative allies. She thought of the United States because of her great financial strength, her appreciable naval power in the Pacific, and her likely value in keeping Great Britain out of the ring: of Germany because of her military power on the Russian frontier; of Great Britain because of her overwhelming naval power. Some held that Great Britain was only approached in the second place. Whether that were so or not, the British Power proved favourable.

Japan was lucky in the moment of her approach. It had become obvious at that time to British statesmanship that the old ideal of "splendid isolation" was no longer tenable. The British Empire needed alliances, or at least safeguarding understandings with other nations. But it almost seemed as though the knowledge had come too late. Apparently there were no European friendships offering. Japan thus found Great Britain in a somewhat anxious mood, and an alliance was concluded between the Power which had hitherto followed a policy of splendid isolation and the *parvenu* Power of the Far East. Japan was now all ready, and Russia was doomed to be ousted from her position as a great Power in the Pacific.

A great deal of nonsense has been written and accepted as true concerning the war between Japan and Russia. Throughout the course of that war the Japanese took the best of care to put their own view of the case before the world. The "wonderful heroism," "the marvellous strategical and tactical skill," "the perfect medical and transport arrangements" of the Japanese forces received something more than their fair share of praise, because of the intelligent and perspicuous industry of the Japanese publicity agencies. The Japanese conducted a fine campaign. Their generals and admirals followed the best models in their dispositions. Both in the movements and in the sanitary regulation of the troops, the commanders were much helped by the habit of discipline of a nation inured to yield blind obedience to a god-born ruler. Still there was no inspired genius for war shown by the Japanese. Their movements were copied from the books. A well-led White army of much less strength would, I believe, have driven them ultimately from Corea into the sea. Their seeming want of power of original thought and their reliance on routine made their movements slow and flabby. They won by the inferiority of the enemy rather than by a great genius for warfare.

The Russians on their side fought under the dispiriting conditions of having a well-trained enemy in front and a revolution behind. The heart of the nation was not with them, and the Russian autocracy was hampered at every turn by the internal disorders of European Russia. It seems probable that the autocracy hoped to solve in part a double problem by the mischievous ingenuity of drafting as many as possible of the discontented at home to the war abroad. That helped things in Russia, but added to the difficulties of the generals in Manchuria. Withal, the Russians put up a good fight. The early engagements were but rearguard actions, the Japanese having an enormous superiority of force, and the Russians striving to delay rather than to arrest their advance. It was not until Mukden that the single line of railway to Russia had brought General Kouropatkin a fair equality of force: and he had to contend then with the tradition of retreat which had been perforce established in his army, and with the growing paralysis of his home government confronted by a great revolutionary movement. Even so, Mukden was a defeat and not a rout.

It is necessary to keep in mind these facts in order to arrive at a sound conclusion as to the future position of Russia in the Pacific. It is not safe to rule her out of the reckoning altogether. A second war, waged by a united Russia against Japan, would probably have a far different result, and would drive Japan off the Asiatic mainland were the ring to be kept clear. For the present, however, Russia is a Power with a great territory washed by the Pacific Ocean, but with no decisive voice in its destinies.

CHAPTER III

THE RISE OF JAPAN

The misfortune of success has never been better exemplified in the world's history than in the results which have followed from the White Man's attempt to arouse Japan to an appreciation of the blessings of European civilisation. Our fathers and grandfathers of the middle nineteenth century battered at the barred and picturesque doors of the land of the Mikado with a vague idea that there was plunder, trade or some other tangible benefit to be got from dragging the quaint Yellow Recluse out of his retirement. Without a foreboding, every civilised Power that had a fighting ship and the time to spare, took some part in urging Japan to awake and be modern. A great deal of gunpowder was burned before the little Asiatic nation stirred. Then she seemed in a flash to learn the whole lesson of our combative civilisation. Naval strategy; the forging of trade-marks; military organisation; appreciation of the value of cheap labour and of machinery in industry; aseptic surgery; resolute and cunning diplomacy—all these were suddenly added to the mental equipment of an Asiatic people, and all used in reprisal against Europe. To-day Japan is the greatest warrior Power in the Pacific, and is also a powerful factor in that war for markets which is not the least important manifestation of race rivalry. As sailors, soldiers, merchants and factory hands, the Japanese are unmistakably awake.

With a discipline impossible of achievement by a European race, the Japanese people pursued the methods of eclectic philosophy in their nation-making. They copied the best from the army systems of Germany and France: duplicated the British naval discipline: adopted what they thought most efficient of the industrial machinery of Europe and America, including a scientific tariff. Nothing that seemed likely to be of advantage was neglected. Even the question of religion was seriously considered, and these awakened people were at one time on the point of a simultaneous national adoption of some form of Christianity. But they were convinced on reflection that nothing of Europe's success in this world was due to religion; and, unconcerned for the moment with anything that was not of this world, decided to forbear from "scrapping" Shintoism and sending it to the rubbish heap where reposed the two-handled sword of the Sumarai.[2]

This miracle of the complete transformation of a race has been accomplished in half a century. Within the memory of some living people the Japanese were content with a secluded life on their hungry islands, where they painted dainty pictures, wove quaint and beautiful fabrics, cultivated children and flowers in a spirit of happy artistry, and pursued

war among themselves as a sport, with enthusiasm certainly, but without any excessive cruelty, if consideration be given to Asiatic ideas of death and the Asiatic degree of sensitiveness to torture. They were without any ideas of foreign conquest. The world had no respect for Japan then. Specimens of Japanese painting and pottery were admired by a few connoisseurs in little corners of the world (such as Bond Street, London), and that was all. Now, Japan having learned the art of modern warfare, we know also that the Japanese are great artists, great philosophers, great poets. Of a sudden a nation has jumped from being naturally chosen as the most absurd and harmless vehicle for a Gilbert satire to that of being "the honoured ally" of Great Britain, in respect to whose susceptibilities that satire should be suppressed.

But our belated respect for the artistry of the Japanese gives little, if any, explanation of the miracle of their sudden transformation. The Chinese are greater artists, greater philosophers, superior intellectually and physically. They heard at an even earlier date the same harsh summons from Europe to wake up. But it was neglected, and, whatever the outcome of the revolutionary movement now progressing, the Chinese are not yet a Power to be taken into present consideration as regards the Pacific Ocean or world-politics generally. The most patient search gives no certain guidance as to the causes of Japan's sudden advance to a position amongst the world's great nations. If we could accurately determine those causes it would probably give a valuable clue to the study of the psychology of races. But the effort is in vain. An analogy is often drawn between the Japanese and the British. Except that both were island races, there are few points of resemblance. The British islands, inhabited originally by the Gauls, had their human stock enriched from time to time by the Romans, the Danes, the Teutons, the Normans. The British type, in part Celtic, in part Roman, in part Danish, in part Anglo-Saxon, in part Norman, was naturally a hard-fighting, stubborn, adventurous race fitted for the work of exploration and colonisation.

But the Japanese had, so far as can be ascertained, little advantage from cross-breeding. Probably they were originally a Tartar race. The primitive inhabitants of the islands were ancestors of the Hairy Ainus, who still survive in small numbers. Like the aboriginals of Australia, the Ainus were a primitive rather than a degraded type, closely allied to the ancestors of the European races. Probably the Tartar invaders who colonised Japan came by way of Corea. But after their advent there was no new element introduced to give the human race in Japan a fresh stimulus; and that original Tartar stock, though vigorous and warlike, has never proved elsewhere any great capacity for organisation.

In the sixth century of the Christian Era, Chinese civilisation and the Buddhistic religion came to the Japanese, who at the time had about the same standard of culture as the Red Indians of the American continent when the *Mayflower* sailed. For some four centuries the Japanese island race was tributary to China, and during that time there was evolved a national religion, Shintoism, which probably represented the old Tartar faith modified by Chinese philosophy. In the eighth and subsequent centuries, Japan in its national organisation very closely resembled feudal Europe. As in Europe, there was a service tenure for the land; a system by which organised groups, or KO's, became answerable collectively for the deeds of each member of the group; and, as in feudal Europe, Church and State made rival claims to supreme power.

Indiscriminate fighting between rival feudal lords, a constant strife between the Shoguns, representing the priestly power, and the Mikados, representing the civil power, make up the islands' history for century after century. Through it all there is no gleam of light on the evolution of the latent powers which were to come to maturity, as in an hour, during the nineteenth century. Japan appeared to be an average example of a semi-civilised country which would never evolve to a much higher state because of the undisciplined quarrelsomeness of its people.

In the sixteenth century Europe first made the acquaintance of Japan. Italian, Portuguese, Dutch, Spanish, British traders and explorers visited the country. St Francis Xavier established missions there and baptized many in the Christian faith. After two centuries of general toleration, with intervals of welcome and yet other intervals of resolute massacre, in 1741 the last of the Europeans were ordered out of the islands, the Japanese having decided that they wanted neither the religion, the trade, nor the friendship of the White Man. The same prohibitions were applied at the same time to Chinese traders. A resolute policy of exclusiveness was adopted.

Japan seems to have learned absolutely nothing from her first contact with European civilisation. She settled down to the old policy of rigorous exclusiveness, and to a renewal of her tribal and religious warfare, in the midst of which, like a strange flower in a rocky cleft, flourished a dainty æstheticism. The nineteenth century thus dawned on Japan, a bitterly poor country, made poorer by the devotion of much of her energies to internal warfare and by the devotion of some of her scanty supply of good land to the cultivation of flowers instead of grain. The observer of the day could hardly have imagined more unpromising material for the making of the modern Japanese nation, organised with Spartan thoroughness for naval, military and industrial warfare.

The United States in 1853 led the way in the successful attempt of White civilisation to open up trade relations with Japan. The method was rude; and it was followed by resolute offers of "friendship," backed by armed threats, from Great Britain, France, Russia and Portugal. The Japanese wanted none of them. The feeling of the people was distinctly anti-foreign. They wished to be left to their flowers and their family feuds. But the White Man insisted. In 1864 a combination of Powers forced the Straits of Shimonoseki. The Japanese were compelled by these and other outrages to a feeling of national unity. In the face of a foreign danger domestic feuds were forgotten. By 1869 Japan had organised her policy on a basis which has kept internal peace ever since (with the exception of the revolt of the Satsuma in 1884), and she had resolved on fighting out with Russia the issue of supremacy in the Pacific. Within a quarter of a century the new nation had established herself as a Power by the sensational defeat, on land and sea, of China. The Peace of Shimonoseki extended her territory to Formosa and the Pescadores, and filled her treasury with the great war indemnity of £57,000,000. She then won, too, a footing on the Asiatic mainland, but was for the time being cheated of that by the interference of Europe, an interference which was not repeated when, later, having defeated Russia in war and having won an alliance with Great Britain, she finally annexed Corea.

From the Peace of Shimonoseki in 1895 the progress of Japan has been marvellous. In 1900 she appeared as one of the civilised Powers which invaded China with a view to impress upon that Empire the duty a semi-civilised Power owed to the world of maintaining internal order. In 1902 she entered into a defensive and offensive alliance with Great Britain, by which she was guaranteed a ring clear from interference on the part of a European combination in the struggle with Russia which she contemplated. The treaty was a triumph of diplomatic wisdom. Appearing to get little, Japan in real truth got all that her circumstances required. A treaty binding Great Britain to come to her aid in any war would have been hopeless to ask for, and not very useful when obtained, for the Japanese attack on Russia might then have been the signal for a general European war in which possibly a European combination would have crippled Great Britain and then turned its united attention to the destruction of Japan's nascent power. A treaty which kept the ring clear for a single-handed struggle with Russia was better than that risk. In return Japan gave nothing in effect except a pledge to make war on her own immediate enemy, Russia, for the assistance of Great Britain if necessity arose.

The conditions created by the Anglo-Japanese treaty of 1902 developed naturally to the Battle of Mukden, the culminating point of a campaign in which for the first time for many years the Yellow Race vanquished the White Race in war. That Battle of Mukden not only established Japan's position in the world. It made the warlike awakening of China inevitable, and restored to the daylight again the long-hidden yet always existing arrogance of Asia. Asia has ever nurtured an insolence beside which any White Race pride is insignificant. That fact is made patent during recurring epochs of history. The Persian Darius sent to the Greeks for earth and water, symbols to acknowledge that "Persia ruled the land and the oceans." The Huns later looked upon the White Men whom they conquered as something lower than animals. The Turks, another great Asiatic race to war against Europe, could compare the White Man only to that unclean beast, the dog. The first European ambassadors who went to China were forced to crawl with abject humility to the feet of the Chinese dignitaries. In his secret heart—of which the European mind knows so little—the Asiatic, whether he be Japanese, Chinese, or Indian, holds a deep disdain for the White. The contempt we feel for them is returned more than one hundredfold.

Mukden brought that disdain out of its slumber. The battle was therefore an event of history more important than any since the fall of Constantinople. For very many years the European hegemony had been unquestioned. True, as late as 1795, Napoleon is credited with having believed that the power of the Grand Turk might be revived and an Ottoman suzerainty of Europe secured. But it was only a dream; more than half a century before that the doom of the Turk, who had been the most serious foe to Christian Europe, was sealed. From 1711 to 1905, whatever questions of supremacy arose among the different European Powers, there was never any doubt as to the superiority of the European race over all coloured races. The White Man moved from one easy conquest to another. In Asia, India, China, Persia and Japan were in turn humbled. Africa was made the slave-farm of the White Race.

Now in the twentieth century at Mukden the White Race supremacy was again challenged. It was a long-dormant though not a new issue which was thus raised. From the times beyond which the memory of man does not stretch, Asia had repeatedly threatened Europe. The struggle of the Persian Empire to smother the Greek republics is the first of the invasions which has been accurately recorded by historians; but probably it had been preceded by many others. The waves of war that followed were many. The last was the Ottoman invasion in the fourteenth century, which brought the banners of Asia right up to the walls of Vienna, swept the Levant of Christian ships, and threatened even the Adriatic; and which has left the

Turk still in the possession of Constantinople. But by the beginning of the eighteenth century the fear of the Turks gaining the mastery of Europe had practically disappeared, and after then the Europeans treated the coloured races as subject to them, and their territories as liable to partition whenever the method of division among rival White nations could be agreed upon.

Mukden made a new situation. The European Powers were prompt to recognise the fact. Doubt even came to Great Britain whether the part she had played as foster-mother to this Asiatic infant of wonderful growth had been a wise one. A peace was practically forced upon Japan, a peace which secured for her at the moment nothing in the way of indemnity, but little in the way of territorial rights, and not even the positive elimination of her enemy from the Asiatic coast. True, she has since won Corea on the basis of that peace and has made secure certain suzerain rights in Manchuria, but this harvest had to be garnered by resolute diplomacy and by maintaining a naval and military expenditure after the war which called for an extreme degree of self-abnegation from her people.

If the present position of affairs could be accepted as permanent, there would be no "problem of the Pacific." That ocean would be Japan's home-water. Holding her rugged islands with a veteran army and navy; so established on the mainland of Asia as to be able to make a flank movement on China; she is the one "Power in being" of the Pacific littoral. But as already stated, the verdict of the war with Russia cannot be taken as final. And soon the United States will come into the Pacific with overwhelming force on the completion of the Panama Canal—an event which is already foreshadowed in a modification of the Anglo-Japanese treaty to relieve Great Britain of the possible responsibility of going to war with America on behalf of Japan. The permanence of the Japanese position as the chief Power of the Pacific cannot therefore be presumed. The very suddenness with which her greatness has been won is in itself a prompting to the suspicion that it will not last. It has been a mushroom growth, and there are many indications that the forcing process by which a Power has been so quickly raised has exhausted the culture bed. In the character of her population Japan is in some respects exceedingly rich. The events of the past few years have shown them to possess great qualities of heroism, patience and discipline. But they have yet to prove that they possess powers of initiative, without which they must fail ultimately in competition with peoples who make one conquest over Nature a stepping-stone to another. And it is not wholly a matter of race prejudice that makes many observers view with suspicion the "staying power" of the character of a nation which thinks so differently from the average European in matters of sex, in commercial honesty, and in the obligations of good faith. Many of those who have travelled in the East, or have done business with Japan, profess a doubt that an enduring greatness can be built upon a national character which runs contrary in most matters to our accepted ideas of ethics. They profess to see in the present greatness of achievement marking Japanese national life a "flash in the pan"—the astonishing precocity and quickness of progress of that type of doomed infant which quickly flowers and quickly fades in the European slums and which is known as "The Mongol" to medical science because of a facial peculiarity which identifies it infallibly. "The Mongol" of European child-life comes to an astonishingly early maturity of brain: its smartness is marvellous. But it is destined always to an early end from an ineradicable internal weakness which is, in some strange way, the cause of its precocious cleverness.

Whether the Japanese cleverness and progressiveness will last or not, the nation has to be credited with them now as a live asset. But apart from the national character the nation possesses little of "natural capital." There is practically no store of precious metals; a poor supply of the useful minerals; small area of good land; and the local fisheries have been exploited with such energy for many generations that they cannot possibly be expanded in productivity now. The statesmen of New Japan have certainly won some overseas Empire as an addition to the resources available for a sound fabric of national greatness. But what has been won is quite insufficient to weigh in the scale against the "natural capital" of almost any of Japan's rivals in the Pacific.

For want of territory to colonise under her own flag, Japan has lost many subjects to alien flags. Japanese settlements of some strength exist on the Pacific coast of America, in the Hawaiian Islands, and in parts of China. There is little doubt that Japanese policy has hoped that in some cases at least her flag would follow her nationals. Talk, not all of it quite irresponsible, has credited Japan with definite designs on many Pacific settlements, especially the Hawaiian Group where her nationals to-day outnumber any other single element of the population. But there are now no islands or territories without a protecting flag. Even when, as was said to be the case with Mexico and another Latin-American country, a weak and friendly nation seems to offer the chance of annexation of territory following a peaceable penetration, there is the power of the United States to interpose a veto. Japan thus cannot add to her natural resources without a war; and she has not, it would seem, sufficient natural resources to back up a war with the enemies she would have to meet now in the Pacific.

If she were to put aside dreams of conquest and Empire, has Japan a sound future in the Pacific as a thriving minor manufacturing and trading power? I must say that it seems to me doubtful. The nation has drunk of the wine of life and could hardly settle down to a humdrum existence. No peaceable policy could allow of a great prosperity, for the reasons of natural poverty already stated. It would be a life of drudgery without the present dream of glory. To study the Japanese emigrant away from his own country is to understand that he has not the patience for such a life. In British Columbia, in California, in Hawaii, the same conclusion is come to by European fellow-residents, that the Japanese worker is arrogant, unruly, unreliable. In Japan itself there are signs that the industrial population will not tolerate for ever a life of very poor living and very hard working if there is not a definite and immediate benefit of national glory promised.

The position of Japan in the Pacific seems to me, then, that she cannot reasonably expect to win in a struggle for its mastery: and yet that she will inevitably be forced to enter into that struggle. A recent report in a Tokio paper stated: "At a secret session of the Budget Commission on February 3, Baron Saito, Minister of Marine, declared that the irreducible minimum of naval expansion was eight battleships of the super-Dreadnought class, and eight armoured cruisers of the same class, which must be completed by 1920, construction being begun in 1913. The cost is estimated at £35,000,000." And the paper (*Asahi Shimbun*) went on to hint at the United States as the Power which had to be confronted. That is only one of very many indications of Japanese national feeling. She has gone too far on the path to greatness to be able to retire safely into obscurity. She must "see it through." Feats of strength far nearer to the miraculous than those which marked her astonishing victory over Russia would be necessary to give Japan the slightest chance of success in the next struggle for the hegemony of the Pacific.

CHAPTER IV

CHINA AND THE TEEMING MILLIONS OF ASIA

China is potentially the greatest Power on the western littoral of the Pacific. Her enormous territory has vast agricultural and mineral resources. Great rivers give easy access to some of the best of her lands. A huge population has gifts of patient labour and craftsmanship that make the Chinaman a feared competitor by every White worker in the world. In courage he is not inferior to the Japanese, as General Gordon found. In intelligence, in fidelity and in that common sense which teaches "honesty to be the best policy," the Chinaman is far superior to the Japanese.

The Chinaman has been outstripped up to the present by the Japanese in the acquirement of the arts of Western civilisation, not because of his inferior mind, but because of his deeper disdain. He has stood aside from the race for world supremacy on modern lines, not as one who is too exhausted for effort, but as one who is too experienced to try. China has in the past experimented with many of the vaunted ideas and methods of the new civilisation, from gunpowder to a peerage chosen by competitive examination, and long ago came to the conclusion that all was vanity and vexation of spirit.

The Chinaman is not humble; not content to take an inferior place in the world. He has all the arrogance of Asia. The name of "Heavenly Kingdom" given to the land by its inhabitants, the grandiose titles assumed by its rulers, the degrading ceremonies which used to be exacted from foreigners visiting China as confessions of their inferiority to the Celestial race, show an extravagant pride of birth. In the thirteenth century, when Confucian China, alike with Christian Europe, had to fear the growing power of the fanatical Mohammedans, a treaty of alliance was suggested between France and China: and the negotiations were broken off because of the claim of China that France should submit to her as a vassal, by way of preliminary. The Chinaman's idea of his own importance has not abated since then. His attitude towards the "foreign devils" is still one of utter contempt. But at present that contempt has not the backing of naval and military strength, and so in practice counts for nothing.

China cherishes the oldest of living civilisations. Her legendary history dates back to 2404 B.C., her actual history to 875 B.C., when a high state of mental culture had been reached, and a very advanced material civilisation also; though some caution is necessary in accepting the statements that at that time China made use of gunpowder, of the mariner's compass, and of printing type. But certainly weaving, pottery, metal-working, and pictorial art flourished. The noble height to which philosophy had reached centuries before the Christian Era is shown by the records of Confucianism and Taoism. Political science had been also cultivated, and there were then Chinese Socialists to claim that "everyone should sow and reap his own harvest."

There seem to have been at least two great parent races of the present population of the Chinese Empire—a race dwelling in the valleys and turning its thoughts to peace and the arts, and a race dwelling on the Steppes and seeking joy in war. It was the Tartar and Mongol tribes of the Steppes which sent wave after wave of attack westward towards Europe, under chiefs the greatest of whom was Gengis Khan. But it was the race of the valleys, the typical Chinese, stolid, patient, laborious, who established ultimate supremacy in the nation, gradually absorbing the more unruly elements and producing modern China with its contempt for military glory. But the Mongols by their wars left a deep impression on the Middle Ages, founding kingdoms which were tributary to China, in Persia, Turkestan and as far west as the Russian Volga.

The earliest record of European relations with China was in the seventh century, when the Emperor Theodosius sent an embassy to the Chinese Emperor. In the thirteenth century Marco Polo visited the Court of the Grand Khan at Pekin, and for a while fairly constant communication between Europe and China seems to have been maintained, the route followed being by caravan across Asia. Christian missionaries settled in China, and in 1248 there is a record of the Pope and the Grand Khan exchanging greetings.

When towards the end of the fourteenth century the Ming dynasty supplanted the Mongol dynasty, communication with Europe was broken off for more than a century. But in 1581 Jesuit missionaries again entered China, and the Manchu dynasty of the seventeenth century at first protected the Christian faith and seemed somewhat to favour Western ideas. But in the next century the Christian missions were persecuted and almost extirpated, to be revived in 1846. Since that date "the mailed fist" of Europe has exacted from the Chinese a forced tolerance of European trade and missions.

But Chinese prejudice against foreign intrusion was given no reason for abatement by the conduct of the European Powers, as shown, for example, in the Opium War of 1840. That prejudice, smouldering for long, broke out in the savage fanaticism of the Boxer outbreak of 1900, which led to a joint punitive expedition by the European Powers, in conjunction with Japan. China had the mortification then of being scourged not only by the "white devils" but also by an upstart Yellow Man, who was her near and her despised neighbour. All China that knew of the expedition to Pekin of 1900 and understood its significance, seems to have resolved then on some change of national policy involving the acceptance of European methods, in warfare at least. Responding to the stimulus of Japan's flaunting of her success in acquiring the ways of the European, China began to consider whether there was not after all something useful to be learned from the Western barbarians. The older Asiatic country has a deep contempt for the younger: but proof of Japan's superior position in the world's estimation had become too convincing to be disregarded. China saw Japan treated with respect, herself with contumely. She found herself humiliated in war and in diplomacy by the upstart relative. The reason was plain, the conclusion equally plain. China began to arm and lay the foundations of a modern naval and military system. The national spirit began to show, too, in industry. Chinese capital claimed its right and its duty to develop the resources of China.

Early in the twentieth century "modern ideas" had so far established themselves in China that Grand Councillor Chang Chih-tung was able, without the step being equivalent to suicide, to memorialise the Throne with these suggestions for reform:—

1. That the Government supply funds for free education.

2. That the Army and Navy be reorganised without delay.

3. That able and competent officials be secured for Government services.

4. That Princes of the blood be sent abroad to study.

5. That arsenals for manufacturing arms, ammunition, and other weapons of war, and docks and shipbuilding yards for constructing warships, be established without delay.

6. That only Chinese capital be invested in railway and mining enterprises.

7. That a date be given for the granting of a Constitution.

Chang Chih-tung may be taken as the representative of the new school of Chinese thought. His book *Chuen Hsueh Pien* (China's Only Hope) is the Bible of the moderate reformers. He states in that book:—

"In order to render China powerful, and at the same time preserve our own institutions, it is absolutely necessary that we should utilise Western knowledge. But unless Chinese learning is made the basis of education, and a Chinese direction given to thought, the strong will become anarchists, and the weak slaves. Thus the latter end will be worse than the former.... Travel abroad for one year is more profitable than study at home for five years. It has been well said that seeing is a hundred times better than hearing. One year's study in a foreign institution is better than three years in a Chinese. Mencius remarks that a man can learn foreign things best abroad; but much more benefit can be derived from travel by older and experienced men than by the young, and high mandarins can learn more than petty officials.... Cannot China follow the *viam mediam*, and learn a lesson from Japan? As the case stands to-day, study by travel can be better done in that country than in Europe, for the following reasons.... If it were deemed advisable, some students could afterwards be sent to Europe for a fuller course."

After the Russian-Japanese War Chinese students went to Japan in thousands, and these students laid the foundation of the Republican school of reformers which is the greatest of the forces striving for mastery in China to-day. The flow of students to Japan was soon checked by the then Chinese Government, for the reason that Republican sentiments seemed to be absorbed in the atmosphere of Japan, despite the absolutism of the Government there. In the United States and in Europe the Chinese scholar was able, however, to absorb Western knowledge without acquiring Republican opinions! There is some suggestion of a grim jest on the part of the Chinese in holding to this view. It recalls Boccaccio's story of the Christian who despaired of the conversion of his Jewish friend when he knew that he contemplated a visit to Rome. The Chinese seemed to argue that a safe precaution against acquiring Republican views is to live in a Republican country. Chinese confidence in the educational advantages offered by the United States has been justified by results. American-educated Chinese are prominent in every phase of the Reform movement in China, except Republican agitation. The first Reform Foreign Minister in China, the first great native Chinese railway builder, the first Chinese women doctors, the greatest native Chinese banker, are examples of American training.

It would be outside the scope of this work to attempt to deal in any way exhaustively with the present position in China. What the ultimate outcome will be, it is impossible to forecast. At present a Republic is in process of formation, after the baby Emperor through the Dowager Empress had promulgated an edict stating:

"We, the Emperor, have respectfully received the following Edict from her Majesty the Dowager:

"In consequence of the uprising of the Republican Army, to which the people in the Provinces have responded, the Empire seethed liked a boiling cauldron, and the people were plunged in misery. Yuan Shih-kai, therefore, commanded the despatch of Commissioners to confer with the Republicans with a view to a National Assembly deciding the form of government. Months elapsed without any settlement being reached. It is now evident that the majority of the people favour a Republic, and, from the preference of the people's hearts, the will of Heaven is discernible. How could we oppose the desires of millions for the glory of one family? Therefore, the Dowager Empress and the Emperor hereby vest the sovereignty in the people. Let Yuan Shih-kai organise with full powers a provisional Republican Government, and let him confer with the Republicans on the methods of establishing a union which shall assure the peace of the Empire, and of forming a great Republic, uniting Manchus, Chinese, Mongols, Mohammedans, and Tibetans."

But all men whom I have met who have had chances of studying Chinese conditions at first hand, agree that the Chinese national character is not favourable to the permanent acceptance of Republican ideas. If there is one thing which seems fixed in the Chinese character it is ancestor-worship, and that is essentially incompatible with Republicanism. [3] But what seems absolutely certain is that a new China is coming to birth. Slowly the great mass is being leavened with a new spirit.

Now a new China, armed with modern weapons, would be a terrible engine of war. A new China organised to take the field in modern industry would be a formidable rival in neutral markets to any existing nation. The power of such a new China put at the disposal of Japan could at least secure all Asia for the Asiatics and hold the dominant position in the Northern Pacific. Possibly it could establish a world supremacy, unless such a Yellow union forced White Races to disregard smaller issues and unite against a common foe. Fortunately a Chinese-Japanese alliance is not at present in the least likely. The Chinese hatred of the Japanese is of long standing and resolute, though it is sometimes dissembled. The Japanese have an ill-concealed contempt for the Chinese. Conflict is more likely than alliance between the two kindred races.

Further, the Chinese will probably move far more slowly on any path of aggression than did the Japanese, for they are intensely pacific. For many

generations they have been taught to regard the soldier as contemptible, the recluse scholar as admirable. Ideas of overseas Empire on their part are tempered by the fanatic wish of every Chinaman that his bones should rest in his native land. It will only be in response to enormous pressure that China will undertake a policy of adventure.

That pressure is now being engendered from within and without. From without it is being engendered by insolent robberies of territory and other outrages on the part of foreign Powers. More particularly of late has the modern arrogance of Japan impressed upon the old-fashioned arrogance of China the fact that the grave scholar, skilled in all the lore of Confucius, is a worthless atom beside a drilled coolie who can shoot straight. From within the pressure is being engendered by the great growth of population. For some time past infanticide has been common in China as a Malthusian check. Now European missionaries seek to discourage that. European medicine further sets itself to teach the Yellow Man to cope with plague, smallpox, and cholera, while European engineering abates the terrors of flood and of crop failure.

Machiavelli would have found prompting for some grim aphorism in this curious eagerness of Europe to teach the teeming millions of Asia to rid themselves of checks on their greater growth, and thus to increase the pressure of the Asiatic surplus seeking an outlet at the expense of Europe. It is in respect to the urgent demand for room for an overcrowding population that there exists alike to China and Japan the strongest stimulus to warlike action in the Pacific. China in particular wants colonies, even if they be only such colonies as provide opportunities for her coolies to amass enough wealth to return in old age to China. From the fertile basin of China there have been overflow waves of humanity ever since there has been any record of history. Before the era of White settlement in the Pacific the Chinese population had pushed down the coast of Asia and penetrated through a great part of the Malay Archipelago, an expansion not without its difficulties, for the fierce Malay objected to the patient Chinaman and often the Chinaman remained to fertilise but not to colonise the alien soil. By some Providential chance neither the Chinaman nor the Japanese ever reached to Australia in the early days of the Pacific, though there are records of Japanese fishermen getting as far as the Hawaiian Group, a much more hazardous journey. If the Asiatics had reached Australia the great island would doubtless have become the southern province of Asia, for its native population could have offered no resistance to the feeblest invader.

In the past, however, the great natural checks kept the Asiatic populations within some limits. Internal wars, famines, pestilences, infanticide—all claimed their toll. Nature exercised on man the checks which exist throughout the whole animal kingdom, and which in some regions of biology are so stern that it is said that only one adult survives of 5,000,000 spawn of a kind of oyster. Now European influence is steadily directed in Asia to removing all obstacles to the growth of population. When the Asiatics wish to fight among themselves Europe is inclined to interfere (as at the time of the Boxer outbreak in China), on the ground that a state of disorder cannot be tolerated. In India internecine warfare is strictly prohibited by the paramount Power. In Japan all local feuds have been healed by pressure from Europe and America, and the fighting power of the people concentrated for external warfare.

Not alone by checking internal warfare does Europe insist on encouraging the growth of the Asiatic myriads. European science suggests railways, which make famine less terrible; flood prevention works which save millions of lives. European moralists make war on such customs as the suicide of young widows and the exposure for death of female children. But, far more efficacious than all, European scientists come forward to teach to the Asiatics aseptic surgery, inoculation, and the rest of the wisdom of preventive and curative medicine. Sometimes Nature is stronger than science. The Plague, for instance, still claims its millions. But even the Plague diminishes before modern medical science.

In his *Health and Empire* (1911), Dr Francis Fremantle tells of the campaign against plague in India. He writes:

"The death-rate from plague in 1904 in the Lahore and Amritsar districts in which I worked was 25 per 1000. Over 1,000,000 Indians died of plague in 1904, over 1,000,000 in 1905; in 1906, 332,000, and it was thought the end was in sight. But 640,000 died in the first four months of 1907; in 1908, 321,000 died; in 1909 only 175,000, but in 1910 again very nearly 500,000, and this year more than ever. The United Provinces had barely been reached by the epidemic in 1904; now with a population equal to that of the United Kingdom, they have been losing 20,000 every week; and the Punjab 34,000 in one week, 39,000, 47,000, 54,000, 60,000 and so on—over 430,000 in the first four months of this year in a population of 25,000,000. Imagine Great Britain and Ireland losing the same proportion—over 1,000,000 from plague in half a year. And India as a whole has in fifteen years lost over 7,000,000 from plague. Why wonder at her unrest?

"What, then, can the Government do? Extermination of rats is impossible; disinfection on a large scale is impracticable; evacuation of villages cannot be done voluntarily on any universal scale; the Government will not apply compulsion, and such evacuation is quite useless without a rigid cordon of police or military that will prevent communication between one infected village and others not yet infected. A cordon, it has been proved over and over again, cannot be maintained; the native who wishes to pass it has only to present some official with a cautious rupee. Extermination of rats in an Asiatic country has often failed; but here is without a shadow of doubt the key to the problem. The methods formerly adopted had been to give a capitation grant for every rat brought to the appointed place, and before long it was found, for instance in Bombay, that an extensive trade had grown up in the breeding of rats, whereby, at a few annas apiece from the Government, many families were able to sustain a comfortable existence.... But since sentence on the rat-flea has been pronounced for the murder of 7,000,000 persons and over, the best method for his extermination will not be far off.

"It is often debated whether even half-measures are worth being continued. Professor W. J. Simpson, in his exhaustive monograph on the plague, and in 1907 in his *Croonian Lectures*, has shown how in history epidemics of plague have come and gone in different countries with long intervals between them, often of one hundred and thirty to one hundred and fifty years. In the eighteenth century, for instance, India seems to have been almost free of the plague, but early in the seventeenth century it suffered severely. The present epidemic is assuming, as far as we can trust previous records, unprecedented proportions; probably after a few years it will die out again.

"An occasional cynic may argue that, since we have saved so many thousands of lives annually from famine and wars, it may be just as well to let the plague take their place. To such a pessimistic and inhuman conclusion it is impossible for one moment to submit. It may be that for economic reasons some parts of the Indian Empire would be happier if their population were less dense; but it does not follow that we should allow Death to stalk uninterrupted, unopposed, and apparently without limit, throughout the country. Economics apart, we may yet be absolutely convinced, whether as doctors or as statesmen, that it is our mission, our duty, to protect the populations included under British rule to the best of our ability against every scourge as it may arise; and therefore it is urgent that such measures as we have be pushed forward with the utmost vigour."

That tells (in a more convincing way, because of the impatience of the doctor, accustomed to European conditions, at the slow result of work in India) how resolute is the White Man's campaign against the Yellow Man's death-rate in one part of Asia. Such a campaign in time must succeed in destroying the disease against which it is directed and thus adding further to the fecundity of Asia.

Nor is the fight against diseases confined to those parts of Asia under direct White rule. The cult of White medicine spreads everywhere, carried by Japanese as well as by European doctors and missionaries. Its effects already show in the enormous increase of Asiatic population, proved wherever definite figures are available. That growth adds year by year to the danger that the Yellow Man will overrun the Pacific and force the White Man to a second place in the ocean's affairs, perhaps not even leaving him that.

An older and sterner school of thought would have condemned as fatuous the White Races' humanitarian nurture of the Yellow Races. But the gentler thought of to-day will probably agree with Dr Fremantle that the White Man cannot "allow Death to stalk uninterrupted, unopposed" even through the territory of our racial rivals. But we must give serious thought to the position which is thus created, especially in view of the "levelling" racial tendency of modern weapons of warfare. China has a population to-day, according to Chinese estimates, of 433,000,000; according to an American diplomatist's conclusions, of not much more than half that total. But it is, without a doubt, growing as it never grew before; and modern reform ideas will continue to make it grow and render the menace of its overflow more imminent.

At present the trend of thought in China is pacific. But it is not possible to be sure that there will not be a change in that regard with the ferment of new ideas. The discussion to-day of a Republic in China, of womanhood suffrage in China, of democratic socialism in China, suggests that the vast Empire, which has been for so long the example of conservative immobility most favoured by rhetoricians anxious to illustrate a political argument, may plunge into unexpected adventures. China has in the past provided great invaders of the world's peace. She may in the near future turn again to the thoughts of military adventure. The chance of this would be increased if in the settlement of her constitutional troubles a long resort to arms were necessary. Then the victorious army, whether monarchical or Republican, might aspire to win for a new China recognition abroad.

It is a fortunate fact that supposing a revival of militancy in China, a revival which is possible but not probable, the first brunt of the trouble would probably fall upon Japan. At the present moment Japan is the most serious offender against China's national pride. As the conqueror of Corea and the occupier of Manchuria, she trespasses most of all foreign Powers on the territories and the rights of China. After Japan, Russia would have to expect a demand for a reckoning; Great Britain would come third and might come into collision with an aggressive China, either because of the existence of such settlements as Hong Kong or because of the Thibetan boundary. A China in search of enemies, however, would find no lack of good pretexts for quarrelling. There are, for instance, the offensive and humiliating restrictions on Chinese immigration of the United States, of Canada, New Zealand and Australia.

I find it necessary, however, to conclude that so far as the near future is concerned, China will not take a great warrior part in the determining of Pacific issues. She may be able to enforce a more wholesome respect for her territorial integrity: she may push away some intruders: she may even insist on a less injurious and contemptuous attitude towards her nationals abroad. But she will not, I think, seek greatness by a policy of aggression. There is no analogy between her conditions and those of Japan at the time of the Japanese acceptance of European arts and crafts. Japan at the time was a bitterly quarrelsome country: she turned from civil to foreign war. China has been essentially pacific for some centuries. Japan was faced at the outset of her national career with the fact that she had to expand her territory or else she could not hope to exist as a great Power. China has within her own borders all that is necessary for national greatness.

If at a later date the Chinese, either from a too-thorough study of the lore of European civilisation, or from the pressure of a population deprived of all Malthusian checks and thus finding an outlet absolutely necessary, should decide to put armies and navies to work for the obtaining of new territory, the peril will be great to the White Man. Such a Chinese movement could secure Asia for the Asiatics, and might not stop at that point. But that danger is not of this decade, though it may have to be faced later by the White Power which wins the supremacy of the Pacific.

CHAPTER V

THE UNITED STATES—AN IMPERIAL POWER

Following the map of the North-Western Pacific littoral, the eye encounters, on leaving the coast of China, the Philippine Islands, proof of the ambition of the United States to hold a place in the Pacific.

It is a common fallacy to ascribe to the United States a Quakerish temperament in foreign affairs. Certain catch-words of American local politics have been given a fictitious value, both at home and abroad. "Republican Simplicity," "The Rights of Man," "European Tyranny," "Imperial Aggression," "The Vortex of Militarism"—from these and similar texts some United State publicists are wont to preach of the tyranny of European kings and emperors; of their greed to swallow up weak neighbours; and of the evils of the military and naval systems maintained to gratify such greed. By much grandiose assertion, or by that quiet implication which is more complete proof of a convinced mind than the most grandiose of assertion, the American nation has been pictured in happy contrast to others, pursuing a simple and peaceful life; with no desire for more territory; no wish to interfere with the affairs of others; in the world, but not of the world.

Astonishment that such professions should carry any weight at all in the face of the great mass of facts showing that the American national temper is exactly the reverse of Quakerish, is modified in the political student by the fact that it is the rule for nations as well as individuals to be judged in the popular estimation by phrases rather than by facts. Ignoring the phrases of politicians and considering only the facts, it will be found that the American people have Imperial ambitions worthy of their ancestry and inseparable from the responsibility towards civilisation which their national greatness involves.

It was in the middle of the eighteenth century that the United States began national housekeeping within a small territory on the seaboard of the Atlantic. By the nineteenth century that area had extended over a section of the continent of America as large almost as Europe. By the twentieth century this Power, still represented as incurably "peaceful and stay-at-home" by its leaders, was established in the Caribbean Sea, on the Isthmus of Panama, in the North and South Pacific, along the coast of Asia, and had set up firmly the principle that whatever affair of the world demanded international attention, from a loan to China, to the fate of an Atlantic port of Morocco, the United States had "interests" which must be considered, and advice which must be regarded. The only circumstance that genuinely suggests a Quaker spirit in United States foreign diplomacy is her quaint directness of language. More effete peoples may wrap every stage of a negotiation up to an ultimatum in honeyed phrases of respect. America "tutoyers" all courts and is mercilessly blunt in claim and warning.

It would be very strange if the United States were otherwise than Imperial in spirit. Nations, like individuals, are affected by biological laws; a young, strong nation is as naturally aggressive and ambitious as a young, strong boy. Contentment with things as they are, a disposition to make anxious sacrifices to the gods who grant peace, are the signs of old age. If a boy is quite good his parents have a reasonable right to suspect some constitutional weakness. A new nation which really resembled what a great many of the American people think the United States to be, would show as a morbid anomaly. No; the course of the world's future history will never be correctly forecasted except on the assumption that the United States is an aggressively Imperial nation, having an influence at least equal to that of any European Power in the settlement of international issues; and determined to use that influence and to extend its scope year by year. In the Problem of the Pacific particularly, the United States must be counted, not merely as a great factor but the greatest factor.

If the American citizen of to-day is considered as though he were a British citizen of some generations back, with a healthy young appetite for conquest still uncloyed, some idea near to the truth will have been reached. But since the deference exacted by public opinion nowadays compels some degree of pretence and does not permit us to parade our souls naked, it is improbable that the United States citizen of this century will adopt the frank freebooting attitude of the Elizabethan Englishman when he was laying the foundations of his Empire by methods inspired somewhat by piracy as well as by patriotism. The American will have to make some concession to the times and seek always a moral sanction for the extension of his boundaries. Such a search, however, is rarely made in vain when it is backed by a resolved purpose. It was sufficient for Francis Drake to know that a settlement was Spanish and rich. The attack followed. The United States needs to know that a possession is foreign, is desirable, and is grossly ill-governed before she will move to a remonstrance in the sacred name of Liberty. Since good government is an ideal which seldom comes at all close to realisation, and the reputation of no form of administration can survive the ordeal of resolute foreign criticism, the practical difference is slight. The American Empire will grow with the benediction always of a high moral purpose; but it will grow.

It is interesting to recall the fact that at its very birth the United States was invested by a writer of prophetic insight with the purple of Empire. Said the *London Gazette* of 1765:—"Little doubt can be entertained that America will in time be the greatest and most prosperous Empire that perhaps the world has ever seen." But the early founders of the new nation, then as now, deceived themselves and others with the view that a pacific little Republic, not a mighty Empire, was their aim. The Imperial instinct showed, however, in the fact that the baby nation had in its youngest days set up a formidable navy. It was ostensibly "for the local defence of its shores," but naval power and overseas Empire are inseparably linked.

The austere Republic began to grow in territory and influence at a rate putting to shame the early feats of the Roman power. By 1893 the United States had made it clear that she would not allow her independence to be fettered in the slightest degree by any claims of gratitude from France: and her Declaration of Neutrality in the European War then raging was a clear statement of claim to be considered as a Power. The war with the Barbary States in 1802 to suppress piracy was a claim to police rights on the high seas, police rights which custom gives only to a paramount sea Power. By the next year Spain and France had been more or less politely relieved of all responsibilities in North America, and the United States stretched from ocean to ocean, and from the Great Lakes to the Gulf of Mexico.

It is upon the early eloquence of her founders as to the duty of the United States to confine her attention strictly to America, that the common misconception of America's place in foreign policy has been built up. That talk, however, was in the first instance dictated largely by prudence. Alexander Hamilton, who controlled the foreign policy of the infant Republic at the outset, was particularly anxious that she should find her feet before attempting any deeds of enterprise. In particular, he was anxious that the United States should not, through considerations of sentiment, be drawn into the position of a mere appanage of France. He set the foundations of what was known afterwards as the "Monroe doctrine," with the one thought that, at the time, a policy of non-interference with European affairs was a necessary condition of free growth for the young nation. The same idea governed Washington's farewell address in 1796 with its warning against "foreign entanglements."

Afterwards the "Monroe doctrine"—deriving its name from a message by President Monroe in 1823—was given the meaning that the United States would not tolerate any interference with the affairs of the American continent by Europe. Finally the "Monroe doctrine," which had begun with an affirmation of America's non-participation in European affairs, and had developed into a declaration against European interference with American affairs, took its present form, which is, in effect, that over all America the United States has a paramount interest which must not be questioned, and that as regards the rest of the world she claims an equal voice with other

Powers. Yet, though that is the actual position, there is still an idea in some minds that the Monroe doctrine is an instrument of humbleness by which the United States claims the immunity of America from foreign interference and guarantees foreign countries from American interference.

It will be of value to recall, in illustration of the rapid growth of an aggressive national pride in the United States, the circumstances which led up to Mr. President Monroe's formal message in 1823. The dawn of the nineteenth century found the young American nation, after about a quarter of a century's existence, fairly on her feet; able to vindicate her rights abroad by a war against the Barbary pirates: given by the cession of Louisiana from France, a magnificent accession of territory. The Empire of Spain was crumbling to pieces, and between 1803 and 1825 the Latin-American Republics in South and Central America were being established on the ruins of that Empire. Spain, her attention engaged in European wars, was able to do little or nothing to assert herself against the rebellious colonies. But in 1815, Napoleon having been vanquished, the Holy Alliance in Europe attempted to reassert the old power of the European monarchies. The terror of Napoleon's army had forced the kings of the earth into a union which forgot national differences and was anxious only to preserve the Divine Right of Kings. The formation of this Holy Alliance was viewed with suspicion and dislike in the United States, and when in 1823 the Alliance raised the question of joint action by European monarchies to restore Spanish rule in South America, the United States responded with Monroe's famous message forbidding any European interference on the continent of America. Such European colonies as already existed would be tolerated, and that was all. The message stated:

> "The American continents by the free and independent conditions which they have assumed are henceforth not to be considered as subjects for future colonisation by any European Power.
>
> "We could not view any interposition for purpose of oppressing them or controlling in any other manner their destiny by any European Power in any other way than as the manifestation of an unfriendly disposition towards the United States."

That "Monroe doctrine" was destined to be extended greatly in scope. In 1845 Mr. President Polk declared that no future European colony should be planted on any part of the North American continent, and laid it down as the duty of the United States "to annex American territory lest it be annexed by European countries." True to that faith, he was responsible for the annexation of Texas, Oregon and California. The United States claim to overlordship of North America was still more remarkably extended in 1867, when a protest was entered against the Federation of the Canadian Provinces. The protest was not insisted upon then, though in 1870 Mr. President Grant revived the spirit of the protest with his forecast of "the end of European political connection with this continent." The Venezuela controversy between Great Britain and the United States in 1895 was responsible for another extension of the Monroe doctrine. It was then claimed that "foreign colonies ought to cease in this hemisphere." Insistence on that would, however, have led to a war in which Great Britain probably would have had the assistance of other European Powers affected; and the Monroe doctrine receded a little.

Exactly how this chief article of the United States foreign policy stands to-day one cannot say. Certainly the Monroe doctrine does not mean, as it was once supposed to mean, that the United States in return for foreign abstention from interference in American affairs pledges herself to keep apart from all extra-American affairs. In world politics she claims and exercises the privileges to which her vast resources and her high state of civilisation are the warrants. In regard to American affairs the Monroe doctrine clearly forbids any further European colonisation in North or South America, and constitutes the United States as the Suzerain Power of all the Latin-American Republics (whether they are willing or not). What else it will be found to mean will depend on the circumstances of the moment and the feelings of the newspaper proprietors who exercise so great an influence on the American man-in-the-street, the governing factor in shaping his country's foreign policy. In European countries, however democratic, the man-in-the-street has rarely any immediate authority over Foreign Affairs. In Great Britain, for example, the questions of the relations of the Government with other countries are not canvassed before the voters. The close oligarchy of the Cabinet (acting often with the Opposition Front Bench) comes to decisions of peace and war, of treaty and *entente*, and, after decision, allows Parliament and the electorate to acquiesce. But in the United States foreign policy is actually dictated by the voters; and that means, in effect, by the newspapers. On occasion the Monroe doctrine has already been interpreted into a notice to quit to all European Powers holding settlements on the American continent. It may in the near future revive that claim to paramount and exclusive authority, and it may cover a declaration of direct suzerainty over Mexico, and over the smaller republics intervening between the United States border and the Panama Canal. In most Latin-American republics disorder is the rule rather than the exception; and it may become at any moment the honest opinion of the man-in-the-street of the United States that the Panama Canal is too important to civilisation to be left to the chances of interference from less stable governments than his own.

These conclusions are inevitable to anyone making any study of American history and the American character. They are not hostile criticisms. They are rather appreciations. A great nation with a belief in its destiny must be "Imperialist" in spirit, because it has a natural desire to spread the blessings of its rule. The people of the United States believe as strongly in themselves as did the ancient Hebrews, and all must have a genuine respect for that fierce spirit of elect nationality which made the Hebrews found a great nation on a goat-patch. In Elizabethan England the same spirit flourished and was responsible for the founding of the British Empire. (It survives still in the British Isles, though somewhat spasmodically.) There is no ground at all either for wonder or for complaint in the fact that Imperialism has been born to vigorous life in the United States, where the people of "God's own country" are firm in these two articles of faith: that any interference in the affairs of the United States is unjust, unnecessary, tyrannical and impious; that any United States interference with another nation is a necessary and salutary effort on behalf of civilisation. Let no man of British blood complain. But let no one in making calculations of world policy be deceived into any other conclusion than that the United States is the great Imperial force of this century, and also the one Power that has enough of the splendid illusions of youth to indulge in crusading wars, for which Europe nowadays is too old and cautious.

In the countries of Europe other than Great Britain that which I have stated is coming to be generally recognised, and if at any time a combination could be proposed with any hope of success "to put America in her place," the combination would be formed and the Old World would grapple with the New to try conclusions. Without Great Britain, however, such an alliance would have at present no chance of success, and British adherence is not within the realm of practical thought to-day.

The Imperialist tendency of United States policy is shown with particular clarity in the history of the Pacific Ocean. Very early in her life the vigorous young nation saw the Fates beckoning her across the Pacific. The downfall of the Spanish power in North America left the United States heir to a great stretch of rich coast line, including the noble province of California. Russia was ousted from the north-west coast of the Continent by a wise purchase. Before then, American whalers sailing out of Boston had begun to exploit the Southern Pacific. Their whaling trips brought back knowledge of the Hawaiian or Sandwich Group, and, following exactly the methods of British colonisation, American missionaries were the pioneers of American nationalisation. As far back as 1820 Hiram Bingham preached his first sermon at Honolulu from the text, "Fear not, for, behold, I bring you glad tidings of great joy." A handsome church now marks the gratitude of his native converts. With equal justice Bingham's American compatriots might have set up a great statue to him as the first warden of the Marches of the Pacific for the United States. For from that day the annexation of Hawaii was inevitable. The process took the familiar course. First the United States Republic exercised a benevolent suzerainty over the Hawaiian kingdom. Then the blessing of free institutions was bestowed on the natives by the foundation of an Hawaiian Republic. The next step was definite annexation. Following that, came steps for the formation of a great naval base at Honolulu.

When I visited the Hawaiian Group in the spring of 1909 the work of fortifying Honolulu was being pushed on with great vigour, and the American military and civil authorities boasted of their intention to make it the Gibraltar of the Pacific. The city of Honolulu has at present a very small harbour, a little bay to which access is given by an opening in the coral reefs which surround the island. This port would hardly afford shelter to a squadron of cruisers. But to the left as one enters is Pearl Harbour, a magnificent stretch of land-locked water sufficient to float a great Fleet. But Pearl Harbour basin in its natural state is too well protected, there being no means of access except for very small boats. American energy is now remedying that, and a deep-water channel is being cut from Honolulu Harbour to Pearl Harbour to take vessels of the largest draught at all tides. When that channel is completed, Pearl Harbour will be at once commodious and easily protected. The single narrow entrance will be dominated by the guns of Malakiki Hill, a great eminence, somewhat like Gibraltar in shape, to the right of the town, which commands the sea-front east and west: and within Pearl Harbour the American Pacific Fleet will find a safe haven. It will be absolutely impregnable from the sea. Hostile ships approaching Honolulu would have to steer straight for Malakiki and then defile amid the coral reefs past its guns before the entrance to Pearl Harbour would open before them.

But land defence has also to be taken into account. The chief male element of the Hawaiian population is not American, not native Hawaiian. It is Japanese. The Mikado's subjects represent now the largest fighting element in the population, outnumbering even the natives. These Japanese, imported as coolies for the sugar-fields, are mostly men of military training. Further influx of them has now been stopped, not under an Immigration Restriction Act, but by private treaty with Japan; and, as a measure of precaution, an Arms Registration Ordinance provides that no citizen shall have in his possession firearms unless he is licensed by the Government. But this precaution would be in vain if Japan ever seriously thought of using her 50,000 soldier-citizens in the Hawaiian Group against the United States; for the whole of the fishing industry is in the hands of the Japanese, and their sampans could land arms at various places on the islands with ease. Such a contingency has been foreseen in the laying out of Honolulu as a naval base, and the land fortifications are designed with the same thoroughness as those designed to beat off a sea attack.

A glance at the map will show that the Power which holds Hawaii with a powerful Fleet can dominate the whole of the Northern Pacific, threatening every point east and west. The American position there is weakened by only one circumstance, the great Japanese population. This, though it may not be recruited with further drafts of males from its native source, will always be a very considerable, if not the most considerable, element of the Hawaiian population, for most of the coolies are married, and the Japanese abroad as well as at home fills the cradle industriously.

I remember on the morning of April 1, 1909, coming into Honolulu city from the Moana Hotel on the sea-beach, I found the tram rushed by Japanese at all the stopping places. Two cruisers of their navy had entered the harbour—cruisers which were once upon a time the Russian *Variag* and *Koreitz*. All Japan in Honolulu was making holiday. A fleet of sampans (the Japanese fishing-vessel) surrounded the ships, which commemorated so signally a great and successful war. The water front was lined with Japanese, the women and children mostly in their national costume. One Japanese father came on to the tram with seven boys, the eldest of whom did not seem more than ten years of age. Asked, he said that they were all his own children. There will never be a lack of a big Japanese population in Hawaii.

The definite acquisition of Hawaii may be fairly dated from 1851. Before then there had been a significant proof of America's gaze turning westward by the appointment in 1844 of Mr Caleb Cushing as the United States Ambassador to the Court of China. A little later (1854) the American Power found the Japanese policy of exclusiveness intolerable, and United States warships broke a way into Japanese ports. It had also been decided by then that the task, originally undertaken by a French Company, of cutting a waterway across the Panama Isthmus should be the responsibility of the United States. British susceptibilities on the point were soothed by the Clayton-Bulwer treaty guaranteeing the neutrality of the canal, a treaty which was subsequently abrogated in response to the increasing deference which the growing power of the American Republic could exact. That abrogation created the present position which gives the United States sole control of that canal, and the right to fortify its entrances.

By the middle of the nineteenth century, therefore, the United States, a Power which some people still insist on regarding as an essentially domestic character interested only in purely American affairs, had established herself in a commanding strategical position in the North Pacific, had constituted herself the arbiter of Japanese national manners, and had obtained the control of the future waterway from the Atlantic to the Pacific. The second half of the same century was destined to see an even more remarkable Imperial expansion. The misgovernment of Cuba by Spain became intolerable to American public opinion, and in 1898 war was declared with the avowed purpose of conferring the blessings of freedom on the people of Cuba. If one accepted the nonsensical view that the United States is a Power lifted above ordinary human nature by some mysterious racial alchemy, it would be difficult to understand why a war to free Cuba should also have been waged in another ocean to acquire the Philippines. But, looking at the matter in a sane light, it was natural that, being engaged in a war with Spain, the United States should strike at Spain wherever a blow was possible and should destroy the Spanish power in the Pacific Ocean as well as in the Caribbean Sea. Besides, the opportunity offered of stretching the arm of America right across the Pacific to the very coast of Asia. The Filipinos did not relish the substitution for the weak rule of Spain of the strong rule of the United States, and American Imperialism had the experience of having to force, by stern warfare on the liberated, acceptance of its rôle of liberator. Perhaps the experience taught it some sympathy with older players at the game of Empire-making: certainly it did not abate its ardour in the good work.

So much for the past history of the United States in the Pacific. A forecast of her influence on the future of the ocean is clearly indicated by the past. The United States spread from the east of the North American continent to the west, because there is no method known to prevent the extension of a highly civilised, a young, an ardent nation at the expense of backward, effete and tired peoples. It was impossible that either the Red Indian tribes or the picturesque old settlements of the Californian Spanish should stand in the way of the American Republic stretching from ocean to ocean. Once the United States was established on the Pacific coast, it was equally inevitable that the arm of her power should stretch across the ocean. The acquisition of the Hawaiian Group was necessary for the sound defence of the coast. The American trading ships which sought the coast of Asia and found barbaric barriers against commerce being battered down by European venturers, had to do as the other White Men did. The flag thus had to follow in the wake of the trade. It was all natural, necessary and ultimately beneficial to civilisation. Equally inevitable will be the future expansion of the United States in the Pacific. The overwhelming strength of her industrial organisation will give her a first call on the neutral markets of the ocean—*i.e.* those markets to which she has the same right of access as her trade rivals. As the tendency shows for the area of those neutral markets to narrow through coming under the domination of various Powers, the United States will seek to extend her domination too. The protection of what she has will enforce the need of acquiring other strategical points. So her Pacific possessions will grow, almost unconsciously, just as the British Empire grew.

CHAPTER VI

GREAT BRITAIN'S ENTRY INTO THE PACIFIC

Off the coast of China at a point where, in a strategical map the "spheres of influence" of Japan and the United States and Germany would impinge, is the island of Hong Kong, the Far East station of the British Empire. Further south, in the Malay Peninsula, is Singapore, standing guard over the entrance to the Indian Ocean. On these two coaling stations British naval power in the North Pacific is based. The abandonment of either of them is unthinkable to-day, yet neither was taken possession of until the nineteenth century—Singapore in 1819, Hong Kong in 1841. In the South Pacific there was shown an even stronger hesitation in acquiring territory.

Why Great Britain entered so reluctantly into the Pacific as a colonising Power may probably be explained by the fact that at the time the ocean came to be exploited British earth hunger had been satiated. The unsuccessful war which attempted to hold the American colonies to the Mother Country, had made her doubtful whether overseas dominions were altogether a blessing and whether the advantage to be gained from them outweighed the responsibilities which their holding entailed. It seemed to be the natural conclusion from the American War of Independence, that once a colony or a group of colonies arrived at the stage of growth which allowed it to be of some use to the Mother Country, the inevitable next development was for it to throw off the bonds of kinship and enter upon a career of independence at the price of an expensive and humiliating war to its parent. Thus, whilst British sailors were to the front in the exploration of the Pacific, British statesmen showed a great reluctance to take any advantage of their discoveries; and it was a series of accidents rather than any settled purpose which planted the Anglo-Saxon race so firmly in this ocean. India, it must be noted, a century ago was a country having very little direct concern with the Pacific. The holding of the Indian Empire did not depend on any position in the Pacific. That situation has since changed, and Great Britain would be forced to an interest in the Pacific by her Indian Empire if she had no other possessions in the ocean.

In an earlier chapter on Japan, something has been written concerning the reasons which would argue for the absence of an Imperial impulse in the Japanese islands and its presence in the British islands. The inquiry then suggested as to the instincts of expansion and dominion which were primarily responsible for the growth of the British Empire is full of fascination for the historian. If it comes to be considered carefully, the

Empire-making of the British people was throughout the result of a racial impulse working instinctively, spasmodically, though unerringly, towards an unseen goal, rather than of a designed and purposeful statesmanship.

The racial origin of the British people dictated peremptorily a policy of oversea adventure, and that adventure led inevitably to colonisation. In the beginning Britain was a part of Gaul, a temperate and fertile peninsula which by right of latitude should have had the temperature of Labrador, but which, because of the Gulf Stream, enjoyed a climate singularly mild and promotive of fecundity. When the separation from the mainland came because of the North Sea cutting the English Channel, the Gallic tribes left in Britain began to acquire, as the fruits of their gracious environment and their insular position, an exclusive patriotism and a comparative immunity from invasion. These made the Briton at once very proud of his country and not very fitted to defend its shores.

With the Roman invasion there came to the future British race a benefit from both those causes. The comparative ease of the conquest by the Roman Power, holding as it did the mastery of the seas, freed the ensuing settlement by the conquerors from a good deal of the bitterness which would have followed a desperate resistance. The Romans were generous winners and good colonists. Once their power was established firmly, they treated a subject race with kindly consideration. Soon, too, the local pride of the Britons affected their victors. The Roman garrison came to take an interest in their new home, an interest which was aided by the singular beauty and fertility of the country. It was not long before Carausius, a Roman general in Britain, had set himself up as independent of Italy, and with the aid of sea-power he maintained his position for some years. The Romans and the Britons, too, freely intermarried, and at the time when the failing power of the Empire compelled the withdrawal of the Roman garrison, the south of Britain was as much Romanised as, say, northern Africa or Spain.

Thus from the very dawn of known history natural position and climate marked out Britain as the vat for the brewing of a strenuous blood. The sea served her "in the office of a wall or of a moat defensive to a house" to keep away all but the most vigorous of invaders. The charm and fertility of the land made it certain that a bold and vigorous invader would be tempted to become a colonist and not be satisfied with robbing and passing on.

With the decay of the Roman Empire, and the withdrawal of the Roman legions to the defence of Rome, the Romanised Britons were left helpless. Civilisation and the growth of riches had made them at once more desirable objects of prey, and less able to resist attack. The province which Rome abandoned was worried on all sides by the incursion of the fierce clans of the north and the west. A decision, ultimately wise, judged by its happy results, but at the moment disastrous, induced some of the harried Britons to call in to their aid the Norsemen pirates, who at the time, taking advantage of the failing authority of Rome, were swarming out from Scandinavia and from the shores of the Baltic in search of booty. The Angles, the Saxons, the Jutes, were willing enough to come to Britain as mercenaries, even more willing to stay as colonists. An Anglo-Saxon wave swept over the greater part of England, and was stopped only by the mountains of Wales or of Scotland. That was the end of the Britons as the chief power in Britain, but they mingled with their conquerors to modify the Anglo-Saxon type with an infusion of Celtic blood. In the mountainous districts the Celtic blood continued to predominate, and does to this day.

The Anglo-Saxons would have been very content to settle down peacefully on the fat lands which had fallen to them, but the piratical nests from which they themselves had issued still sent forth broods of hungry adventurers, and the invasions of the Danes taught the Anglo-Saxons that what steel had won must be guarded by steel. They learned, too, that any race holding England must rely upon sea-power for peaceful existence. After the Danish, the last great element in the making of the present British race, was the Norman. The Normans were not so much foreigners as might be supposed. The Anglo-Saxons of the day were descendants of sea-pirates who had settled in Britain and mingled their blood with the British. The Normans were descendants of kindred sea-pirates who had settled in Gaul, and mingled their blood with that of the Gauls and Franks. The two races, Anglo-Saxon and Normans, after a while combined amicably enough, the Anglo-Saxon blood predominating, and the British type was evolved, in part Celtic, in part Danish, in part Anglo-Saxon, in part Norman—a hard-fighting, stubborn adventurous race, which in its making from such varied elements had learned the value of compromise, and of the common-sense principle of give-and-take. One can see that it was just the race for the work of exploration and colonisation.

When this British people, thus constituted, were driven back to a sea-frontier by the French nation, it was natural that they should turn their energies overseas. To this their Anglo-Saxon blood, their Danish blood, their Norman blood prompted. The Elizabethan era, which was the era of the foundation of the British Empire overseas, was marked by a form of patriotism which was hard to distinguish in some of its manifestations from plain robbery. The fact calls for no particular condemnation. It was according to the habit of thought of the time. But it is necessary to bear in mind that the hunt for loot and not the desire for territory was the chief motive of the flashing glories of the Elizabethan era of seamanship; for that is the explanation why there was left as the fruit of many victories few permanent settlements.

Drake was the first English naval leader to penetrate to the Pacific. His famous circumnavigation of the world is one of the boldest exploits of history. Drake's log entry on entering the Pacific stirs the blood:

"Now, as we were fallen to the uttermost parts of these islands on October 28, 1578, our troubles did make an end, the storm ceased, and all our calamities (only the absence of our friends excepted) were removed, as if God all this while by His secret Providence had led us to make this discovery, which being had according to His will, He stayed His hand."

On this voyage Drake put in at San Francisco, which he named New Albion. He went back to Europe through the East Indies and around Africa. But Drake made no attempt at colonisation. Looting of the Spanish treasure ships was the first and last object of his cruise. What was, according to our present lights, a more honourable descent upon the Pacific was that of Admiral Anson in the eighteenth century. He, in 1740, took a Fleet round the stormy Horn to subdue the Philippines and break the power of Spain in the Pacific. The force thought fitting for such an enterprise in those days was 961 men! Anson did not subdue the Philippines; but they were guarded by the scurvy, which attacked the English Fleet, rather than by the Spanish might, and the little disease-racked English squadron was able to cripple the Spanish power in the Pacific by the mere dread of its presence. Anson took prizes and made them masquerade before the enemy's coast as hostile warships, and paralysed the Spanish commerce in those seas. He returned to England with only 335 men out of his original complement of 961. Practically all the deaths had been from disease. But again the idea of the Pacific expedition was not to colonise but to strike a blow at a rival European Power. It was not until the nineteenth century that Great Britain established herself on the western flank of the North Pacific.

So far as the South Pacific was concerned British indifference was complete, and it was shared by other nations. In the days when the fabled wealth of the Indies was the magnet to draw men of courage and worth to perilous undertakings by sea and land, there was nothing in the South Pacific to attract their greed, and nothing, therefore, to stimulate their enterprise. The Spaniard, blundering on America in his quest for a western sea-passage to the ivory, the gold, and the spices of India, found there a land with more possibilities of plunder than that which he had originally sought. He was content to remain, looting the treasuries of the Mexicans and of the Peruvians for metals, and laying the forests of Central America under contribution for precious woods. He ventured but little westward, and the Hawaiian Islands represented for a time the extreme western limit of his adventures. Following him for plunder came the English, and they too were content to sweep along the western coast of South America without venturing further towards the unknown west.

From another direction the sea-route to India was sought by Portuguese, and Dutch, and English and French. Groping round the African coast, they came in time to the land of their desires, and found besides India and Cathay, Java, the Spice Islands, and other rich groups of the Malay Archipelago. But they, just as the Spaniards, did not venture west from South America; and neither Portuguese, Dutch, French nor English set the course of their vessels south from the East Indies.

It was thus Australia remained for many years an unknown continent. And when at last navigators, more bold or less bound to an immediate greed, touched upon the shores of Australia, or called at the South Sea Islands, they found little that was attractive. In no case had the simple natives won to a greed for gold and silver, and so they had no accumulations of wealth to tempt cupidity. In the case of Australia the coast-line was dour and forbidding, and promised nothing but sterility.

The exploring period in which the desire for plunder was the chief motive passed away, having spared the South Pacific. It was therefore the fate of Australia, of New Zealand, and of most of the islands of Polynesia and Melanesia, to be settled under happier conditions, and to be spared the excesses of cruelty which marked the European invasion of the West Indies and the Americas. The Newest World began its acquaintance with civilisation under fairly happy auspices.

It was not until the middle of the seventeenth century that a scientific expedition brought the South Pacific before the attention of Britain. A transit of Venus across the sun promised to yield valuable knowledge as to the nature of solar phenomena. To observe the transit under the best conditions, astronomers knew that a station in the South Seas was necessary, and Lieutenant Cook, R.N., an officer who had already distinguished himself in the work of exploration, was promoted to be Captain and entrusted to lead a scientific expedition to Otaheite. Added to his commission was an injunction to explore the South Seas if time and opportunity offered. Captain Cook was of the type which makes time and opportunity. Certainly there was little in the equipment of his expedition to justify an extension of its duties after the transit of Venus had been duly observed. But he took it that his duty was to explore the South Seas, and explore them he did, incidentally annexing for the British Empire the Continent of Australia.

That was in 1770. But still there was so little inviting in the prospect of settlement in the South Seas that it was some eighteen years before any effort was made to follow up by colonisation this annexation by Captain Cook. When the effort was made it was not on very dignified lines. The American colonies had at one time served as an outlet for the overflow of the British prisons. The War of Independence had closed that channel. The overcrowding of the British prisons became desperate, and, because it was necessary to find some relief for this—not because it was considered advantageous to populate the new possession—the First Fleet sailed for the foundation of Australia in 1788.

We shall see in subsequent chapters how the reluctance of the governing Power of the British race in the Home Country to establish an Empire in the South Pacific found a curious response in the stubborn resoluteness of the colonists who settled in Australia and New Zealand to be more English than the English themselves, to be as aggressively Imperialistic almost as the men of the Elizabethan era. (What might almost be called the "Jingoism" of the British nations in the South Pacific must have a very important effect in settling the mastery of that ocean.) In the present chapter the establishment of the British Power in the North Pacific chiefly will be considered.

Singapore is to-day the capital of the three Straits Settlements—Singapore, Penang, and Malacca, but it is the youngest of the three settlements. Malacca is the oldest. It was taken possession of by the Portuguese under Albuquerque in 1511, and held by them until 1641, when the Dutch were successful in driving them out. The settlement remained under the Government of the Dutch till 1795, when it was captured by the English, and held by them till 1818, at which date it was restored to the Dutch, and finally passed into British hands in pursuance of the treaty with Holland of 1824. By that treaty it was arranged that the Dutch should leave the Malay Peninsula, the British Government agreeing at the same time to leave Sumatra to the Dutch. When Malacca was taken possession of by the Portuguese in 1511, it was one of the great centres for the commerce of the East; but under Dutch rule it dwindled, and Penang acquired a monopoly of the trade of the Malayan Peninsula and Sumatra, together with a large traffic with China, Siam, Borneo, the Celebes, and other places in the Archipelago. When Singapore was established Penang in its turn had to yield the first place to the new city.

Singapore was acquired for Britain by Sir Stamford Raffles in 1819, by virtue of a treaty with the Johore princes. It was at first subordinate to Bencoolen in Sumatra, but in 1823 it was placed under the Government of Bengal; it was afterwards incorporated in 1826, with Penang and Malacca, and placed under the Governor and Council of the Incorporated

Settlements. Singapore is now one of the great shipping ports of the world, served by some fifty lines of steamers, and with a trade of over 20,000,000 tons a year. The harbour of Singapore is fortified, and the port is indicated by one advanced school of British Imperialists as the future chief base of a Fleet, contributed to by India, Australia, New Zealand, South Africa, and Canada, and kept to a standard of strength equal to that available to any other two Powers in the Pacific. Captain Macaulay, in a strategical scheme for Imperial Defence which has been received with deep attention in Great Britain, suggests:—

"The influence which an Indian Ocean Fleet, based on Colombo and Singapore, would have on Imperial Defence can hardly be exaggerated. The Indian Ocean—a British Mediterranean to the Pacific—with its openings east and west in our hands, is a position of readiness for naval action in the Western Pacific, the South Atlantic, or the Mediterranean. In the first case it influences the defence of Canada and the Australasian States; in the second, that of South Africa. An Indian Ocean Fleet can reinforce, or be reinforced by the Fleets in European waters, if the storm centre be confined to Europe or to the Pacific. As regards the direct naval defence of the Australasian Provinces, no better position could be chosen than that of a Fleet based on Singapore, with an advanced base at Hong Kong, because it flanks all possible attack on them. An advanced flank defence is better than any direct defence of so large a coast-line as that of Australia from any point within it. Moreover, Singapore and Hong Kong are much nearer to the naval bases of any Powers in the Western Pacific than those countries are to Australia or to Canada. Hence, in operations for the defence of any Province, they favour offensive-defensive action on our part. And offensive-defensive is the great characteristic of naval power. Any East Asian Power contemplating aggression against Australasian or North American territory must evidently first deal with the Indian Ocean Fleet.

"It is impossible to ignore the strategical and political significance of the Imperial triangle of India based on South Africa and the Australasian States, and its influence in the solution of the new problems of Imperial Defence. The effective naval defence of the self-governing Provinces is best secured by a Fleet maintained in the North Indian Ocean; and the reinforcement of the British garrison in India is best secured by units of the Imperial Army maintained in the self-governing Provinces. If these two conditions are satisfied, the problem of the defence of the Mother Country is capable of easy solution."

Hong Kong is of less strategical importance than Singapore. But it is marked out as the advanced base of British naval power in the North Pacific. It has one of the most magnificent harbours in the world, with an area of ten square miles. The granite hills which surround it rise between

2000 and 3000 feet high. The city of Victoria extends for four miles at the base of the hills which protect the south side of the harbour, and contains, with its suburbs, 326,961 inhabitants. It is the present base of the China squadron, and is fortified and garrisoned.

As already stated, the conditions which some years ago made the mastery of the Pacific unimportant to India no longer exist, and the safety of the Indian Empire depends almost as closely on the position in the Pacific as the safety of England does on the position in the Atlantic. But, except by making some references in future chapters on strategy and on trade to her resources and possibilities, I do not propose to attempt any consideration of India in this volume. That would unduly enlarge its scope. In these days of quick communication, both power and trade are very fluid, and there is really not any country of the earth which has not in some way an influence on the Pacific. But so far as possible I have sought to deal only with the direct factors.

Having noted the British possessions in the North Pacific, it is necessary to turn south and study the young "nations of the blood" below the Equator before estimating British Power in the Pacific.

CHAPTER VII

THE BRITISH CONTINENT IN THE PACIFIC

Those who seek to find in history the evidence of an all-wise purpose might gather from the fantastic history of Australasia facts to confirm their faith. Far back in prehistoric ages, this great island was cut adrift from the rest of the world and left lonely and apart in the Southern Pacific. A few prehistoric marsupials wandered over its territory and were hunted by poor nomads of men, without art or architecture, condemned by the conditions of their life to step aside from the great onward current of human evolution.

Over this land the winds swept and the rains fell, and, volcanic action having ceased, the mountains were denuded and their deep stores of minerals bared until gold lay about on the surface. Coal, copper, silver, tin, and iron too, were made plentifully accessible. At the same time enormous agricultural plains were formed in the interior, but under climatic conditions which allowed no development of vegetable or animal types without organised culture by a civilised people.

Nature thus seemed to work consciously for the making of a country uniquely fitted for civilisation by a White Race, whilst at the same time ensuring that its aboriginal inhabitants should not be able to profit by its betterment, and thus raise themselves to a degree of social organisation which would allow them to resist an invading White Race. In the year when Captain Cook acquired the Continent of Australia for Great Britain, it was ripe for development by civilised effort in a way which no other territory of the earth then was; and yet was so hopelessly sterile to man without machinery and the other apparatus of human science, that its aboriginal inhabitants were the most forlorn of the world's peoples, living a starveling life dependent on poor hunting, scanty fisheries and a few roots for existence.

It needs no great stretch of fancy to see a mysterious design in the world-history of Australia. Here was a great area of land stuffed with precious and useful minerals, hidden away from the advancing civilisation of man as effectually as if it had been in the planet Mars. In other parts of the globe great civilisations rose and fell—the Assyrian, the Egyptian, the Chinese, the Greek, the Roman,—all drawing from the bowels of the earth her hidden treasures, and drawing on her surface riches with successive harvests. In America, the Mexican, Peruvian and other civilisations learned to gather from the great stocks of Nature, and built up fabrics of greatness from her rifled treasures. In Australia alone, amid dim, mysterious forests, the same prehistoric animals roamed, the same poor nomads of men lived and died, neither tilling nor mining the earth—tenants in occupation, content with a bare and accidental livelihood in the midst of mighty riches.

Australia too was not discovered by the White Man until the moment when a young nation could be founded on the discovered principles of Justice. To complete the marvel, as it would seem, Providence ordained that its occupation and development should be by the one people most eminently fitted for the founding of a new nation on the virgin soil.

The fostering care of Nature did not end there. The early settlers coming to Australia not only found that nothing had been drawn from the soil or reef, that an absolutely virgin country was theirs to exploit, but also were greeted by a singularly happy climate, free of all the diseases which afflicted older lands. Prolific Australia, with all its marvellous potentialities, lay open to them, with no warlike tribes to enforce a bloody beginning to history, no epidemics to war against, no savage beasts to encounter. And they were greeted by an energising climate which seemed to encourage the best faculties of man, just as it gave to harvests a wonderful richness and to herds a marvellous fecundity.

How it came to be that such a vast area of the earth's surface, so near to the great Indian and Chinese civilisations, should have so long remained unknown, it is difficult to understand. There is faint evidence that the existence of the great Southern continent was guessed at in very early days, but no attempt at exploration or settlement was made by the Hindoos or the Chinese. When the Greeks, who had penetrated to India under Alexander the Great, returned to their homes, they brought back some talk of a continent south from India, and the later Greek literature and some Latin writers have allusions to the tale. Marco Polo (thirteenth century), during his voyages to the East Indies, seems to have heard of a Southern continent, for he speaks of a Java Major, a land much greater than the isle of Java (which he knew), and which was probably either New Guinea or Australia. On a fifteenth-century map of the world now in the British Museum there are indications of a knowledge of the existence of Australia; and it is undoubtedly included in a map of the world of the sixteenth century.

But there was evidently no curiosity as to the suspected new continent. Australia to-day contains not the slightest trace of contact with ancient or Middle Ages civilisation. Exploration was attracted to the East Indies and to Cathay by the tales of spices, scents, gold, silver, and ivory. No such tales came from Australia. It was to prove the greatest gold-producing country of the world, but its natives had no hunger for the precious metal, though it was strewn about the ground in great lumps in some places. Nor did sugar, spice, and ivory come from the land; nor, indeed, any product of man's industry or Nature's bounty. Wrapped in its mysterious grey-green forests, protected by a coast-line which appeared always barren and inhospitable, Australia remained unknown until comparatively modern times.

In 1581 the Spaniards, under Magalhaes, reached the Philippine Islands by sailing west from the South American coast. In the nature of things their ships would have touched the coast of Australia. In 1606 De Quiros and De Torres reached some of the Oceanian islands, and named one *Terra Austrialia del Espiritu Santo"*, (the Southern Land of the Holy Spirit). As was the case with Columbus in his voyage of discovery to America, De Quiros had not touched the mainland, but his voyage gave the name "Australia" to the new continent.

The English were late in the work of exploring the coast of Australia, though as far back as 1624 there is a record of Sir William Courteen petitioning King James I. for leave to plant colonies in "Terra Australis." In 1688, William Dampier, in the *Cygnet*, touched at the north-western coast of Australia. The next year, in H.M.S. *Roebuck*, he paid a visit to the new land, and, on returning to England, put on record his impressions of its fauna and flora. It was in 1770 that Captain Cook made the first landing at Botany Bay.

The British nation at the time could find no use for Australia. Annexed in 1770 it was not colonised until 1787, when the idea was adopted of using the apparently sterile and miserable Southern continent as a depôt for enforced exiles. It was a happy chance that sent a "racketty" element of British social life to be the first basis of the new Australian population. The poachers, English Chartists, Irish Fenians, Scottish land rebels (who formed the majority of the convicts sent to Australia) were good as nation-building material.

There was work to do there in the Pacific, there is further work in the future, which calls for elements of audacity, of contempt for convention, which are being worked out of the average British type. There could be no greater contrast between, say, a London suburbanite, whose life travels along an endless maze of little gravel paths between fences and trimly-kept hedges, and the Australian of the "back country," who any day may ride out solitary on a week's journey into a great sun-baked wilderness, his life and that of his dog and his two horses dependent on the accurate finding of a series of water-holes: his joy in existence coming from the solitude and the desert, the companionship of his three animals, his tobacco, and the thought of his "mate" somewhere, whom he would meet after six months' absence with a handshake and a monosyllable by way of greeting, and yet with the love of a fond brother.

That London suburbanite gives the key to his kindly and softly sentimental character in his subscription to a society which devotes itself to seeing that the suburban house cat is not left shut up without food when a family goes away on holidays. That Australian shows how far he has reverted to the older human type of relentless purpose when, in the pursuit of his calling, he puts ten thousand sheep to the chance of death from thirst. It is not that he is needlessly cruel, but that he is sternly resolute. The same man would share his last water with his dog in the desert to give both an equal chance of life. He feels the misery of beasts but says nothing, and allows it to interfere nothing with his purpose.

There is a story of a clergyman coming to a back-country station in Australia during the agony of a great drought. He asked of the squatter permission to hold prayers for rain in the woolshed. The squatter turned on him, fiercely gripping him by the arm.

"Listen!" he cried.

From all around came the hoarse, pitiful lowing and bleating of thousands of animals dying of thirst and hunger.

"Listen! If the Almighty does not hear *that*, will he hear us?"

That is the type of man, bred from the wilder types of the British race, who is the backbone of the Australian population, and who will be the backbone of the resistance which the White Man will make to any overflow of Asia along the Pacific littoral.

The Australian took instinctively to his task in the work of White civilisation—that of keeping the Asiatic out of Australia. In the early days of the goldfields, the Chinese began to crowd to the continent, and some squatters of those days designed to introduce them as cheap and reliable shepherds. The mass of the White population protested, with riot and rebellion in some cases. At one time it seemed as though the guns of British warships would fire on Australian citizens in vindication of the right of Chinese to enter Australia. But maternal affection was stronger than logic. The cause of "White Australia" had its way; and by poll taxes and other restrictive legislation any great influx of Asiatics was stopped. At a later date the laws regarding alien immigration were so strengthened that it is now almost impossible for a coloured man to enter Australia as a colonist, even though he be a British subject and a graduate of Oxford University.

Around the ethics of the "White Australia" policy there has raged a fierce controversy. But it is certain that, without that policy, without an instinctive revolt on the part of the Australian colonists against any intrusion of coloured races, Australia would be to-day an Asiatic colony, still nominally held, perhaps, by a small band of White suzerains, but ripe to fall at any moment into the hands of its 10,000,000 or 20,000,000 Asiatic inhabitants.

Instead of that, Australia is at once the fortress which the White Race has thinly garrisoned against an Asiatic advance southward, and the most tempting prize to inspire the Asiatic to that advance. There is not the least doubt that, given Australia, Japan could establish a power threatening the very greatest in Europe. Her fecund people within a couple of generations would people the coast-line and prepare for the colonisation of the interior. Rich fields and rich mines put at the disposal of a frugal and industrious people would yield enormous material wealth.

An organised China would put the island continent to even greater use. But there Australia is, held by a tiny White population, which increases very slowly (for men and women have the ideas of comfort and luxury which lead to small families), but which is now fairly awake to the fact that on the bosom of the Pacific and along its shores will be fought the great race battles of the future.

It is curious for the peoples of Europe, accustomed to associate extreme democracy and socialistic leanings with ideals of pacificism and "international brotherhood," to observe the warlike spirit of the Australian peoples. There are no folk more "advanced" in politics. Their ideal is frankly stated to be to make a "working man's Paradise" of the continent. Yet they are entering cheerfully on a great naval expenditure, and their adoption of a system of universal training for military service provides the only instance, except that of Switzerland, where the responsibility of national defence is freely accepted by the citizen manhood of the nation.

Universal training for military service in Australia, legally enforced in 1909, was made inevitable in 1903, when in taking over the administration of the defences the first Commonwealth Government provided in its Defence Act for the levying of the whole male population for service in case of war. That provision was evidence of the wholesome and natural view taken by Australians of the citizen's duty to his nation. It was also evidence of an ignorance of, or a blindness to, the conditions of modern campaigning. Raw levies, if equipped with courage and hardihood, could be of almost immediate usefulness in the warfare of a century ago. To-day they would be worse than useless, a burden on the commissariat, no support in the field. The logical Australian mind was quick to recognise this. Within five years it was established that, admitting a universal duty to serve, a necessary sequence was universal training for service.

One argument the Australian advocates of universal service had not to meet. In that pioneer country the feeling which is responsible for a kind of benevolent cosmopolitanism, and finds expression in Peace Societies, had little chance of growth. The direct conflict with Nature had brought a sense of the reality of life's struggle, of its reality and of its essential beauty. There is no maundering horror of the natural facts of existence. Australian veins when scratched bleed red blood, not a pale ichor of Olympus. The combative instinct is recognised as a part of human nature, a necessary and valuable part. That defencelessness is the best means of defence would never occur to the Australian as being anything but an absurd idea. He recognises the part which the combative instinct has played, the part it still must play in civilisation: how in its various phases it has assisted man in his upward path; how it has still some part to play in the preservation and further evolution of civilisation.

The original fighting instinct was purely brutal—a rough deadly scramble for food. But it undoubtedly had its value in securing the survival of the best types for the propagation of the species. With its first great refinement, in becoming the fight for mateship, the combative instinct was still more valuable to evolution. The next step, when fights came to be for ideas, marked a rapid growth of civilisation. Exclude chivalry, patriotism, Imperialism, from the motives of the world, and there would never have been a great civilisation.

A distinguished British statesman spoke the other day of the expenditure on armaments as possibly a sign of "relapsing into barbarism." He might more truly have described it as an insurance against barbarism—at once a sign of the continued existence of the forces which made civilisation, and a proof that the advanced races are prepared to guard with the sword what they have won by the sword. The Pacific has seen the tragedy of one nation which, having won to a suave and graceful civilisation, came to utter ruin through the elimination of the combative instinct from its people. The Peruvians had apparently everything to make life happy: but because they had eliminated the fighting instinct their civilisation was shattered to fragments in a year by the irruption of a handful of Spaniards.

The Australian feels that safety and independence must be paid for with strength, and not with abjectness. He does not wish to be another Peruvian: and he builds up his socialistic Utopia with a sword in one hand as was built a temple of Jerusalem.

Some doubt having arisen in the Australian mind, after a system of universal training had been adopted, whether the scheme of training was sufficient, the greatest organiser of the British Army, Field Marshal Lord Kitchener, was asked to visit the Commonwealth and report on that point.

His report suggested some slight changes, which were promptly adopted, but on the whole he approved thoroughly of the proposed scheme, though it provided periods of training which seem startlingly small to the European soldier. But Lord Kitchener agreed, as every other competent observer has agreed, that the Australian is so much of a natural soldier owing to his pioneering habit of life, that it takes but little special military discipline to make him an effective fighting unit.

Committed to a military system which will, in a short time, make some 200,000 citizens soldiers available in case of need, Australia's martial enthusiasm finds expression also in a naval programme which is of great magnitude for so small a people. In July 1909, an Imperial Conference on Defence met in London, and the British Admiralty brought down certain proposals for Imperial naval co-operation. *Inter alia*, the British Admiralty memorandum stated:—

"In the opinion of the Admiralty, a Dominion Government desirous of creating a Navy should aim at forming a distinct Fleet unit; and the smallest unit is one which, while manageable in time of peace, is capable of being used in its component parts in the time of war.

"Under certain conditions the establishment of local defence flotillas, consisting of torpedo craft and submarines, might be of assistance in time of war to the operations of the Fleet, but such flotillas cannot co-operate on the high seas in the wider duties of protection of trade and preventing attacks from hostile cruisers and squadrons. The operations of Destroyers and torpedo-boats are necessarily limited to the waters near the coast or to a radius of action not far distant from a base, while there are great difficulties in manning such a force and keeping it always thoroughly efficient.

"A scheme limited to torpedo craft would not in itself, moreover, be a good means of gradually developing a self-contained Fleet capable of both offence and defence. Unless a naval force—whatever its size—complies with this condition, it can never take its proper place in the organisation of an Imperial Navy distributed strategically over the whole area of British interests.

"The Fleet unit to be aimed at should, therefore, in the opinion of the Admiralty, consist at least of the following: one armoured cruiser (new *Indomitable* class, which is of the *Dreadnought* type), three unarmoured cruisers (*Bristol* class), six destroyers, three submarines, with the necessary auxiliaries such as depôt and store ships, etc., which are not here specified.

"Such a Fleet unit would be capable of action not only in the defence of coasts, but also of the trade routes, and would be sufficiently powerful to deal with small hostile squadrons, should such ever attempt to act in its waters.

"Simply to man such a squadron, omitting auxiliary requirements and any margin for reliefs, sickness, etc., the minimum numbers required would be about 2300 officers and men, according to the Admiralty scheme of complements.

"The estimated first cost of building and arming such a complete Fleet unit would be approximately £3,700,000, and the cost of maintenance, including upkeep of vessels, pay, and interest and sinking fund, at British rates, approximately £600,000 per annum.

"The estimated cost of the officers and men required to man the ships does not comprise the whole cost. There would be other charges to be provided for, such as the pay of persons employed in subsidiary services, those undergoing training, sick, in reserve, etc.

"As the armoured cruiser is the essential part of the Fleet unit, it is important that an *Indomitable* of the *Dreadnought* type should be the first vessel to be built in commencing the formation of a Fleet unit. She should be officered and manned, as far as possible, by Colonial officers and men, supplemented by the loan of Imperial officers and men who might volunteer for the service. While on the station the ship would be under the exclusive control of the Dominion Government as regards her movements and general administration, but officers and men would be governed by regulations similar to the King's Regulations, and be under naval discipline. The question of pay and allowances would have to be settled on lines the most suitable to each Dominion Government concerned. The other vessels, when built, would be treated in the same manner.

"It is recognised that, to carry out completely such a scheme as that indicated, would ultimately mean a greater charge for naval defence than that which the Dominions have hitherto borne; but, on the other hand, the building of a *Dreadnought* (or its equivalent), which certain Governments have offered to undertake, would form part of the scheme, and therefore, as regards the most expensive item of the shipbuilding programme suggested, no additional cost to those Governments would be involved.

"*Pari passu* with the creation of the Fleet unit, it would be necessary to consider the development of local resources in everything which relates to the maintenance of a Fleet. A careful inquiry should be made into the shipbuilding and repairing establishments, with a view to their general adaptation to the needs of the local squadron. Training schools for officers and men would have to be established; arrangements would have to be made for the manufacture, supply, and replenishment of the various naval, ordnance, and victualling stores required by the squadron.

"All these requirements might be met according to the views of the Dominion Governments, in so far as the form and manner of the provision made are concerned. But as regards shipbuilding, armaments, and warlike stores, etc., on the one hand, and training and discipline in peace and war, on the other, there should be one common standard. If the Fleet unit maintained by a Dominion is to be treated as an integral part of the Imperial forces, with a wide range of interchangeability among its component parts with those forces, its general efficiency should be the same, and the facilities for refitting and replenishing His Majesty's ships, whether belonging to a Dominion Fleet or to the Fleet of the United Kingdom, should be the same. Further, as it is a *sine quâ non* that successful action in time of war depends upon unity of command and direction, the general discipline must be the same throughout the whole Imperial service, and without this it would not be possible to arrange for that mutual co-operation and assistance which would be indispensable in the building up and establishing of a local naval force in close connection with the Royal Navy. It has been recognised by the Colonial Governments that, in time of war, the local naval forces should come under the general directions of the Admiralty."

The Commonwealth of Australia representatives accepted in full the proposals as set forth in the Admiralty memorandum. It was agreed that the Australian Fleet unit thus constituted should form part of the Eastern Fleet of the Empire, to be composed of similar units of the Royal Navy, to be known as the China and the East Indies units respectively, and the Australian unit.

The initial cost was estimated to be approximately:

1 armoured cruiser (new *Indomitable* £2,000,000 class).
3 unarmoured cruisers (*Bristols*) at 1,050,000 £350,000.
6 destroyers (*River* class) at £80,000 480,000
3 submarines (*C* class) at £55,000 165,000

Total £3,695,000

The annual expenditure in connection with the maintenance of the Fleet unit, pay of personnel, and interest on first cost and sinking fund, was estimated to be about £600,000, to which amount a further additional sum would have to be added in view of the higher rates of pay in Australia and the cost of training and subsidiary establishments, making an estimated total of £750,000 a year.

The Imperial Government, until such time as the Commonwealth could take over the whole cost, offered to assist the Commonwealth Government by an annual contribution of £250,000 towards the maintenance of the complete Fleet unit; but the offer was refused, and the Australian taxpayer took on the whole burden at once.

Still not content, the Australian Government arranged for a British Admiral of standing to visit the Commonwealth and report on its naval needs. His report suggested the quick construction of a Fleet and of docks, etc., involving an expenditure, within a very short time, of £28,000,000. There was no grumbling at this from the Labour Party Government then in power. "We have called in a doctor. We must take his prescription," said one of the Australian Cabinet philosophically.

The Australian, so aggressive in his patriotism, so determined in his warlike preparations, so fitted by heredity and environment for martial exploits, is to-day the greatest factor in the Southern Pacific. His aggressiveness, which is almost truculence, is a guarantee that the British Empire will never be allowed to withdraw from a sphere into which it entered reluctantly. It will be necessary to point out in a future chapter how the failure, so far, of the Australian colonists to people their continent adequately constitutes one of the grave dangers to the British Power in the Pacific. That failure has been the prompting for much criticism. It has led to some extraordinary proposals being put forward in Great Britain, one of the latest being that half of Australia should be made over to Germany as a peace offering! But, apart from all failures and neglect of the past (which may be remedied for the future: indeed are now in process of remedy), Australia is probably potentially the greatest asset of the British race. Her capacity as a varied food producer in particular gives her value. There is much talk in the world to-day of "places in the sun." Claims founded on national pride are put forward for the right to expand. Very soon there must be a far more weighty and dangerous clamour for "places at table," for the right to share in the food lands of the Earth. Populations begin to press against their boundaries. Modern science has helped the race of man to reach numbers once considered impossible. Machinery, preventive medicine, surgery, sanitation, all have helped to raise vastly his numbers. The feeding of these increasing numbers becomes with each year a more difficult problem. Territories do not stretch with populations. Even the comparatively new nation of the United States finds her food supply and raw material supply tightening, and has just been checked in an attempt to obtain a lien on the natural resources of the British Dominion of Canada. Now, excluding manufactures, the 4½ million people of Australia produce wealth from farm and field and mine to the total of £134,500,000 a year. Those 4½ millions could be raised to 40 millions without much lessening of the average rate of production (only mining and forestry would be affected).

The food production possibilities of Australia make her of enormous future importance. They make her, too, the object of the bitterest envy on the part of the overcrowded, hungry peoples of the Asiatic littoral. The Continent must be held by the British race. It would appear to be almost as certain that it must be attacked one day by an Asiatic race.

CHAPTER VIII

NEW ZEALAND AND THE SMALLER BRITISH PACIFIC COLONIES

A thousand miles east of Australia is another aggressive young democracy preparing to arm to the teeth for the conflict of the Pacific, and eager to embark upon a policy of forward Imperialism on its own account: with aspirations, indeed, to be made overlord of all the Pacific islands under the British Flag.

New Zealand had a softer beginning than Australia, and did not win, therefore, the advantages and disadvantages springing from the wild type of colonists who gave to the Australian Commonwealth a sturdy foundation. Nor has New Zealand the "Bush" conditions which make the back-country Australian quite a distinct type of white man. On those hot plains of Australia, cruel to a first knowledge, very rich in profit and welcome to the man who learns their secrets, most potent of attraction with familiarity and mastery, Nature exacts from man a resolute wooing before she grants a smile of favour. But, once conquered, she responds with most generous lavishness. In return, however, she sets her stamp on the men who come to her favour, and they show that stamp on their faces. Thin, wiry, with deep-set peering eyes, they suggest sun-dried men. But whilst leaching out the fat and softness from them, Nature has compensated the "Bush" Australians with an enduring vitality. No other men, probably, of the world's peoples could stand such strain of work, of hunger, of thirst. No men have finer nerves, greater courage. They must dice with Death for their lives, time and again staking all on their endurance, and on the chance of the next water-hole being still unparched. This gives them a contempt of danger, and some contempt of life, which shows in a cruel touch in their character.

Imagine a white man who, keeping all his education and maintaining his sympathy with modern science and modern thought, withal reverts in some characteristics to the type of the Bedouin of the desert, and you have the typical Australian Bushman. He is fierce in his friendships, stern in his enmities, passionately fond of his horse, so contemptuous of dwellings that he will often refuse to sleep in them, Arabian in his hospitality, fatalistic in his philosophy. He has been known to inflict torture on a native whom he suspects of concealing the whereabouts of a water-hole, and yet will almost kill himself to get help for a mate in need. He is so independent that he hates working for a "boss," and will rarely take work on wages, preferring to live as his own master, by hunting or fossicking, or by undertaking contract work for forest clearing.

There is material for a great warrior nation in these Bushmen, with their capacity for living anyhow, their deadliness as shots, their perfect command of the horse, their Stoic cruelty which would enable them to face any hardship without flinching, and to inflict any revenge without remorse.

New Zealand has not the "Bushman" type. But as some compensation, the early New Zealand settlers had the advantage of meeting at the very outset an effective savage. The Australian learned all his hardihood from Nature; the New Zealand colonist had the Maori to teach him, not only self-reliance but community reliance. Whilst Nature was very kind to him, sparing the infliction of the drought, giving always a reasonable surety of food, he was obliged to walk warily in fear of the powerful and warlike Maori tribes. The phenomenon, so frequent in Australia, of a squatter leading his family, his flocks, and his herds out into the wilderness and fighting out there, alone, a battle with Nature was rare in New Zealand. There the White settlers were forced into groups by the fear of and respect for the Maoris. From the first they knew the value of a fortified post. Until a very late period of their history they saw frequently the uniforms of troops from Great Britain helping them to garrison the towns against the natives.

As was the case with Australia, the British Empire was very reluctant to assume control of New Zealand. Captain Cook, who annexed Australia in 1770, had visited New Zealand in 1769, but had not acquired it formally for the British Crown. The same explorer returned to New Zealand several years after. But from the date of his last departure, 1776, three decades passed before any White settlement was attempted. In 1788 the colonisation of Australia was begun, but it was not until 1814 that a small body of Europeans left Sydney and settled in New Zealand. The Rev. Samuel Marsden, who had been Chaplain to the Convict Colony of New South Wales, was the leader of the band, and its mission was to Christianise the natives. A little later the Wesleyan Church founded a Mission in the same neighbourhood. In 1825 a Company was formed in London to colonise New Zealand, and it sent away a band of pioneers in the ship *Rosanna*. The wild mien of the natives so thoroughly frightened these colonists that almost all of them returned to England. Desultory efforts at settlement followed, small bands of British subjects forming tiny stations at various points of the New Zealand coast, and getting on as well as they might with the natives, for they had no direct protection from the British Government, which was entirely opposed to any idea of annexing the group. There was no fever for expansion in England at the time. The United States had broken away. Canada seemed to be on the point of secession. The new settlement in Australia promised little. But the hand of the British Government was destined to be forced in the matter, and, willy-nilly, Britain had to take over a country which is now one of her most valued possessions.

Mr Edward Gibbon Wakefield was responsible for forcing on the British Government the acquisition of New Zealand. The era was one of philanthropy and keen thought for social reform in Great Britain. The doctrines of the French Revolution still reverberated through Europe, and the rights of humanity were everywhere preached to men confronted with the existence of great social misery, which seemed to deny to the majority of mankind even the degree of comfort enjoyed by animals. Wakefield's remedy was the emigration of the surplus population of the British islands—well, the British islands except Ireland, to which country and its inhabitants Wakefield had an invincible antipathy. The prospectus of the Company to colonise New Zealand stated:

"The aim of this Company is not confined to mere emigration, but is directed to colonisation in its ancient and systematic form. Its object is to transplant English society with its various graduations in due proportions, carrying out our laws, customs, associations, habits, manners, feelings—everything of England, in short, but the soil. We desire so now to cast the foundations of the colony that in a few generations New Zealand shall offer to the world a counterpart of our country in all the most cherished peculiarities of our own social system and national character, as well as in wealth and power."

In due time twelve ships carrying 1125 people sailed for New Zealand. That was the beginning of a steady flow of emigrants mostly recruited by various Churches, and settled in groups in different parts of the New Zealand islands—members of the Free Church of Scotland at Otago, of the Church of England at Canterbury, men of Devon and Cornwall men at New Plymouth.

The British Government could hardly shake off all responsibility for these exiles. But it did its best to avoid annexation, and even adopted the remarkable expedient of recognising the Maoris as a nation, and encouraging them to choose a national standard. The Maori Flag was actually flown on the high seas for a while, and at least on one occasion received a salute from a British warship. But no standard could give a settled polity to a group of savage tribes. The experiment of setting up "The Independent Tribes of New Zealand" as a nation failed. In 1840, Great Britain formally took over the New Zealand islands from the natives under the treaty of Waitangi, which is said to be the only treaty on record between a white race and a coloured race which has been faithfully kept to this day.

"This famous instrument," writes a New Zealand critic, "by which the Maoris, at a time when they were apparently unconquerable, voluntarily ceded sovereign rights over their country to Queen Victoria, is practically the only compact between a civilised and an uncivilised race which has been regarded and honoured through generations of difficulties, distrust, and even warfare. By guaranteeing to the Maori the absolute ownership of their patrimonial lands and the enjoyment of their ancestral rights and customs, it enabled them to take their place as fully enfranchised citizens of the British Empire, and to present the solitary example of a dark race surviving contact with a white, and associating with it on terms of mutual regard, equality and unquestioned loyalty. The measure of this relationship is evident from the fact that Maori interests are represented by educated natives in both houses of the New Zealand Parliament and in the Ministry. The strict observance of the Treaty of Waitangi is part and parcel of the national faith of the New Zealanders, and a glorious monument to the high qualities of one of the finest races of aboriginal peoples the world has ever seen."

The New Zealand colonists, having won the blessing of the British Flag, were not well content. Very shortly afterwards we find Mr James Edward FitzGerald writing to Wakefield, who was contemplating a trip to New Zealand.

"After all, this place is but a village. Its politics are not large enough for you. But there are politics on this side the world which would be so. It seems unquestionable that in the course of a very few years—sometimes I think months—the Australian colonies will declare their independence. We shall live to see an Australasian Empire rivalling the United States in greatness, wealth and power. There is a field for great statesmen. Only yesterday I was saying, talking about you, that if you come across the world it must be to Australia; just in time to draw up the Declaration of Independence."

But that phase passed. New Zealand to-day emulates Australia in a fervent Imperial patriotism, and at the 1911 Imperial Conference her Prime Minister, Sir Joseph Ward, was responsible for the following proposal which was too forward in its Imperialism to be immediately acceptable to his fellow delegates:

"That the Empire has now reached a stage of Imperial development which renders it expedient that there should be an Imperial Council of State, with representatives from all the self-governing parts of the Empire, in theory and in fact advisory to the Imperial Government on all questions affecting the interests of his Majesty's Dominions oversea."

He urged the resolution on the following grounds:

(1) Imperial unity; (2) organised Imperial defence; (3) the equal distribution of the burden of defence throughout the Empire; (4) the representation of self-governing oversea Dominions in an Imperial Parliament of defence for the purpose of determining peace or war, the contributions to Imperial defence, foreign policy as far as it affects the Empire, international treaties so far as they affect the Empire, and such other Imperial matters as might by agreement be transferred to such Parliament.

In advocating his resolution Sir Joseph Ward made an interesting forecast of the future of the British nations whose shores were washed by the Pacific. He estimated that if the present rate of increase were maintained, Canada would have in twenty-five years from now between 30,000,000 and 40,000,000 inhabitants. In Australia, South Africa, and New Zealand the proportionate increase could not be expected to be so great, but he believed that in twenty-five years' time the combined population of those oversea Dominions would be much greater than that of the United Kingdom. Those who controlled the destinies of the British Empire would have to consider before many years had passed the expansion of these oversea countries into powerful nations, all preserving their own local autonomy, all being governed to suit the requirements of the people within their own territory, but all deeply concerned in keeping together in some loose form of federation to serve the general interests of all parts of the Empire.

At a later stage, in reply to Sir Wilfrid Laurier, Prime Minister of Canada, Sir Joseph Ward indulged in an even more optimistic prophecy. The United States, he said, had something like 100,000,000 people. The prospective possibility of Canada for settlement purposes was not less than that of the United States, and the Dominion was capable of holding a population of 100,000,000 in the future. Australia also was capable of holding a similar number, although it would necessarily be a great number of years before that position was reached. South Africa, too, could hold 100,000,000 people. It was no exaggeration to suggest that those three Dominions were capable of holding 300,000,000 of people with great comfort as compared with certain overcrowded countries. New Zealand, in the opinion of many well-qualified men, could carry upwards of 40,000,000 people with comparative ease and comfort.

But these figures are hardly scientific. Climatic and other considerations will prevent Canada from reaching quite the same degree of greatness as the United States. British South Africa could "hold" 100,000,000 people, but it could not support them on present appearances. The possibilities of Australian settlement are difficult to be exaggerated in view of the steady dwindling of the "desert" area in the light of recent research and exploration, and of the fact that all her area is blessed with a genial climate.

New Zealand, to keep 40,000,000 people, would need, however, to have a density of 400 people per square mile, a density surpassed to-day in Belgium and Holland but not reached by Great Britain. A fairly conservative estimate of the possibilities of the British Empire would allow it for the future a white population of 200,000,000, of whom at least half would be grouped near the shores of the Pacific. Presuming a British Imperial Federation on Sir Joseph Ward's lines with such a population, and the mastery of the Pacific would be settled. But that is for the future, the far future.

Sir Joseph Ward, in the event, was not able to carry the Imperial Conference with him, the majority of the delegates considering that the time had not yet come for the organisation of an Imperial Federal system. But it is possible that with the passing of time and the growth of the population of the Dominions overseas, some such system may evolve: and a British Empire Parliament may sit one day at Westminster, at Vancouver or at Sydney. Certainly the likelihood is that the numerical balance of the British race will shift one day from the Atlantic to the Pacific.

Following Australia's example, New Zealand has adopted a system of universal training for military service, but there are indications that she will not enforce it quite so rigorously as her neighbour. In the matter of naval defence, at the Conference of 1909 the New Zealand attitude was thus defined by her Prime Minister:—

"I favour one great Imperial Navy with all the Overseas Dominions contributing, either in ships or money, and with naval stations at the self-governing Dominions supplied with ships by and under the control of the Admiralty. I, however, realise the difficulties, and recognise that Australia and Canada in this important matter are doing that which their respective Governments consider to be best; but the fact remains that the alterations that will be brought about upon the establishment of an Australian unit will alter the present position with New Zealand.

"New Zealand's maritime interests in her own waters, and her dependent islands in the Pacific would, under the altered arrangements, be almost entirely represented by the Australian Fleet unit, and not, as at present, by the Imperial Fleet. This important fact, I consider, necessitates some suitable provision being made for New Zealand, which country has the most friendly feeling in every respect for Australia and her people, and I am anxious that in the initiation of new arrangements with the Imperial Government under the altered conditions, the interests of New Zealand should not be over-looked. I consider it my duty to point this out, and to have the direct connection between New Zealand and the Royal Navy maintained in some concrete form.

"New Zealand will supply a *Dreadnought* for the British Navy as already offered, the ship to be under the control of and stationed wherever the Admiralty considers advisable.

"I fully realise that the creation of specific units, one in the East, one in Australia, and, if possible, one in Canada, would be a great improvement upon the existing condition of affairs, and the fact that the New Zealand *Dreadnought* was to be the flag-ship of the China-Pacific unit is, in my opinion, satisfactory. I, however, consider it is desirable that a portion of the China-Pacific unit should remain in New Zealand waters, and I would suggest that two of the new "Bristol" cruisers, together with three destroyers and two submarines, should be detached from the China station in time of peace and stationed in New Zealand waters; that these vessels should come under the flag of the Admiral of the China unit; that the flagship should make periodical visits to New Zealand waters; and that there should be an interchange in the service of the cruisers between New Zealand and China, under conditions to be laid down.

"The ships should be manned, as far as possible, by New Zealand officers and men, and, in order that New Zealanders might be attracted to serve in the Fleet, local rates should be paid to those New Zealanders who enter, in the same manner as under the present Australian and New Zealand agreement, such local rates being treated as deferred pay.

"The determination of the agreement with Australia has, of necessity, brought up the position of New Zealand under that joint agreement. I therefore suggest that on completion of the China unit, the present agreement with New Zealand should cease, that its contribution of £100,000 per annum should continue and be used to pay the difference in the rates of pay to New Zealanders above what would be paid under the ordinary British rate. If the contribution for the advanced rate of pay did not amount to £100,000 per annum, any balance to be at the disposal of the Admiralty.

"The whole of this Fleet unit to be taken in hand and completed before the end of 1912, and I should be glad if the squadron as a whole would then visit New Zealand on the way to China, leaving the New Zealand detachment there under its senior officer."

From the difference between the naval arrangements of Australia and New Zealand can be gathered some hints of the difference between the national characteristics of the two young nations. Australia is aggressively independent in all her arrangements: loyal to the British Empire and determined to help its aims in every way, but to help after her own fashion and with armies and navies recruited and trained by herself. New Zealand, with an equal Imperial zeal, has not the same national self-consciousness and is willing to allow her share of naval defence to take the form of a cash payment. Probably the most effective naval policy of New Zealand would be founded on a close partnership with Australia, the two nations combining to maintain one Fleet. But that New Zealand does not seem to desire. She is, however, content to be a partner with Australia in one detail of military administration. The military college for the training of officers at the Australian Federal capital is shared with New Zealand. The present Prime Minister of Australia, Mr Fisher, is taking steps towards securing a closer defence bond with New Zealand.[4]

In an aspiration towards forward Imperialism, New Zealand is fully at one with Australia. But she has the idea that the control of the Southern Pacific, outside of the continent of Australia, is the right of New Zealand, and dreams of a New Zealand Empire embracing the island groups of Polynesia. It will be one of the problems of the future for the British Power to restrain the exuberant racial pride of these South Pacific nations, who see nothing in the European situation which should interfere with a full British control of the South Pacific.

In addition to Australia and New Zealand, the British Empire has a number of minor possessions in the South Pacific. In regard to almost all of them, the same tale of reluctant acceptance has to be told. New Guinea was annexed by the Colony of Queensland, anxious to set on foot a foreign policy of her own, in 1883. The British Government repudiated the annexation, and in the following year reluctantly consented to take over for the Empire a third of the great island on condition that the Australian States agreed to guarantee the cost of the administration of the new possession. The Fiji Group was offered to Great Britain by King Thakombau in 1859, and was refused. Some English settlers then began to administer the group on a system of constitutional government under Thakombau. It was not until 1874 that the British Government accepted these rich islands, and then somewhat ungraciously and reluctantly, influenced to the decision by the fact that the alternative was German acquisition.

It was no affectation of coyness on the part of the successive British Governments which dictated a refusal when South Pacific annexations were mooted. Time after time it was made clear that the Home Country wanted no responsibilities there. Yet to-day, as the result mainly of the impulse of Empire and adventure in individual British men, the British Flag flies over the whole continent of Australia, Tasmania, New Zealand, a part of New Guinea, Fiji, and the Ellice, Gilbert, Kermadec, Friendly, Chatham, Cook, and many other groups. It is a strange instance of greatness thrust upon a people.

CHAPTER IX

THE NATIVE RACES

The native races of the South Pacific, with the possible exception of the Maori, will have no influence in settling the destiny of the ocean. Neither the Australian aboriginal nor the Kanaka—under which last general title may be grouped all the tribes of Papua, the Solomons, the New Hebrides and other Oceanic islands—will provide the foundation of a nation. It is one of the curiosities of world-history that no great race has ever survived which had its origin in a land south of the Equator. From the earliest civilisations to the latest, there is not a single instance of a people of the southern hemisphere exercising any notable effect on the world's destinies. Sometimes there seems no adequate reason for this. That Africa north of the Equator should have produced a great civilisation, which was the early guide and instructor of the European civilisations, may be explained in part by the curious phenomenon of the Nile delta, a tract of land the irrigation of which at regular intervals by mysterious natural forces prompted inquiry, and suggested that all the asperities of Nature could be softened by effort. (The spirit of inquiry and the desire for artificial comfort are the great promptings to civilisation.) But it is difficult to understand why in America the aboriginal Mexicans should have been so much more warlike than the Peruvians or any other people in South America; and why the West Pacific should wash with its northern waters the lands of two great races, and with its southern waters flow past lands which, though of greater fertility, remained almost empty, or else were peopled by childlike races, careless of progress and keen only to enjoy the simple happiness offered by Nature's bounty.

The Australian aboriginal race is rapidly dwindling: one of its branches, that which populated the fertile and temperate island of Tasmania, is already extinct. In Tasmania, reacting to the influence of a mild and yet stimulating climate, a climate comparable with that of Devon in England, but more sunny, the Australasian native had won to his highest point of development. Apparently, too, he had won to his highest possible point, for there is evidence that for many generations no progress at all had been made towards civilisation. Yet that point was so low in the stage of evolution that it was impossible for the poor natives to take any part, either as a separate race, or by mingling their blood with another race, in the future of the Pacific. The black Australian is a primitive rather than a degraded man. Most ethnologists have concluded that this black Australian is a Caucasian. Wallace ascribes to him kinship with the Veddas and the

Ainus of Asia. Stratz takes the Australian as the prototype of all the races of man. Schoetensack contends that the human race had its origin in the Australian continent.

But, however dignified by ancestry, the Australian aboriginal was pathetically out of touch with modern civilisation. He broke down utterly at its advent, not so much because of his bad qualities as because of his childishness. Not only were alcohol, opium and greed strange to him, but also weapons of steel and horses and clothing. He had never learnt to dig, to build, to weave. War organisation had not been thought of, and his tribal fights were prodigal of noise but sparing of slaughter. When the White Man came, it was inevitable that this simple primitive should dwindle from the face of the earth. It is not possible to hold out any hope for the future of the Australian blacks. They can never emulate the Maoris of New Zealand, who will take a small share in the building up of a nation. All that may be hoped for is that their certain end will be kept back as long as is humanly possible, and that their declining days will be softened by all kindness. A great reserve in the Northern Territory—a reserve from which the White population would be jealously excluded, and almost as jealously the White fashions of clothing and house-building—holds out the best hope for their future. It is comforting to think that the Australian Government is now resolved to do all in its power for the aboriginals. Indeed, to be just, authority has rarely lacked in kindness of intention; it has been the cruelty of individuals acting in defiance of authority, but aided by the supineness of authority, that has been responsible for most of the cruelty.

The Maori or native New Zealander was of a different type. The Maori was an immigrant to New Zealand. Some time back there was an overflow of population from the fertile sub-tropical islands of Malaysia. A tribe which had already learned some of the arts of life, which was of a proud and warlike character, took to the sea, as the Norsemen did in Europe, and sought fresh lands for colonisation. Not one wave, but several, of this outflow of colonists struck New Zealand. The primitive people there, the Morioris, could offer but little resistance to the warlike Malaysians, and speedily were vanquished, a few remnants finding refuge in the outlying islets of the New Zealand group. Probably much the same type of emigrant occupied Hawaii at one time, for the Hawaiian and the Maori have much in common. But whilst the perpetual summer of Hawaii softened and enervated its colonists, the bracing and vigorous climate of New Zealand had a precisely opposite effect. The dark race of the Pacific reached there a very high state of development.

The Maori system of government was tribal, and there does not seem to have been, up to the time of the coming of the White Man, any attempt on the part of one chief to seize supreme power and become king. Land was held on a communal system, and cultivated fairly well. Art existed, and was applied to boat-building, to architecture, to the embroidering of fabrics, to the carving of stone and wood. War was the great pastime, and cannibalism was customary. Probably this practice was brought by the Maoris from their old home. If it had not been, it might well have sprung up under the strange conditions of life in the new country, for New Zealand naturally possessed not a single mammal, not a beast whose flesh might be eaten. There were birds and lizards, and that was all. The Maoris brought with them dogs, which were bred for eating, but were too few in number to provide a satisfactory food-supply; and rats, which were also eaten. With these exceptions there was no flesh food, and the invitation to cannibalism was clear.

A more pleasant feature of the national life of the Maori was a high degree of chivalry. In war and in love he seems to have had very much the same ideas of conduct as the European of the Age of Chivalry. He liked the combat for the combat's own sake, and it is recorded as one of the incidents of the Maori War that when a besieged British force ran short of ammunition, the Maori enemy halved with them their supply, "so as to have a fair fight."

In his love affairs the Maori was romantic and poetic. His legends and his native poetry suggest a state of society in which there was a high respect for women, who had to be wooed and won, and were not the mere chattels of the men-warriors. Since this respect for womenkind is a great force for civilisation, there is but little doubt that, if the Maoris had been left undisturbed for a few more centuries, they would have evolved a state of civilisation comparable with that of the Japanese or the Mexicans.

When Captain Cook visited New Zealand in 1769 the Maori race probably numbered some 100,000. The results of coming into contact with civilisation quickly reduced that number to about 50,000. But there was then a stay in the process of extinction. The Maori began to learn the virtues as well as the vices of civilisation. "Pakeha" medicine and sanitation were adopted, and the Maori birth-rate began to creep up, the Maori death-rate to decrease. It is not probable that the Maori race will ever come to such numbers as to be a factor of importance in the Pacific. But it will have some indirect influence. Having established the right to grow up side by side with the White colonists, possessing full political and social rights, the Maoris will probably modify somewhat the New Zealand national type. We shall see in New Zealand, within a reasonable time, a population of at least 10,000,000 of people, of whom perhaps 1,000,000 will be Maoris. The effect of this mixture of the British colonising type with a type somewhat akin to the Japanese will be interesting to watch. In all probability New

Zealand will shelter a highly aggressive and a fiercely patriotic nation in the future (as indeed she does at present).

The Malay States bred a vigorous and courageous race of seamen, and Malay blood has been dispersed over many parts of the Pacific, Malays probably providing the chief parent stock both for the Hawaiians and the Maoris. But the Malay Power has been broken up to such an extent that a Malay nation is now impossible. Since the British overlordship of the Malay Peninsula, the Chinese have been allowed free access to the land and free trading rights; and they have ousted the original inhabitants to a large extent.

The Maori excepted, no race of Polynesia or Melanesia will survive to affect the destinies of the Pacific Ocean. Nature was cruelly kind to the Kanaka peoples in the past, and they must pay for their happiness now. In the South Pacific islands, until White civilisation intruded, the curse of Adam, which is that with the sweat of the brow bread must be won, had not fallen. Nature provided a Garden of Eden where rich food came without digging and raiment was not needed. Laughing nations of happy children grew up. True, wars they had, and war brought woe. But the great trouble, and also the great incentive to progress of life, they had not. There was no toiling for leave to live. Civilisation, alas! intrudes now, more urgent each year, to bring its "blessings" of toil, disease, and drabness of fettered life; and the Paradise of the South Sea yields to its advance—here with the sullen and passionate resentment of the angry child, there with the pathetic listlessness of the child too afraid to be angry. But, still, there survives in tree and flower, bird and beast, and in aboriginal man, much that has the suggestion rather of the Garden of Eden than of this curious world which man has made for himself—a world of exacting tasks and harsh taskmasters, of ugly houses and smoke-stained skies, of machinery and of enslaving conventions.

With the White Man came sugar plantations and cotton fields. The Kanaka heard the words "work" and "wages." He laughed brightly, and went on chasing the butterfly happiness. To work a little while, for the fun of the thing, he was willing enough. Indeed, any new sort of task had a fascination for his childish nature. But steady toil he abhorred, and for wages he had no use.

Some three years ago I watched for an hour or two, from the veranda of a house at Suva, a Fijian garden-boy at work. This was a "good" garden-boy, noted in the town for his industry. And he played with his work with an elegant naïveté that was altogether charming to one who had not to be his paymaster. Almost bare of clothing, his fine bronzed muscles rippled and glanced to show that he had the strength for any task if he had but the will.

Perhaps the gentleness of his energy was inspired by the æsthetic idea of just keeping his bronze skin a little moist, so as to bring out to the full its satin grace without blurring the fine anatomical lines with drops of visible sweat. His languid grace deserved that it should have had some such prompting. If a bird alighted on a tree, the Fijian quickly dropped his hoe and pursued it with stones, which—his bright smile said—were not maliciously meant, but had a purpose of greeting. An insect, a passing wayfarer, the fall of a leaf, a cloud in the sky, all provided equally good reasons for stopping work. Finally, at three a little shower came, and the "model boy" of Fijian industry thankfully ceased work for the day.

A gracious, sweet, well-fed idleness was Nature's dower to the Pacific Islander, until the White Man came with his work, as an angel with a flaming sword, and Paradise ended. Now the fruit of that idleness is that the Kanaka can take no part in the bustling life of modern civilisation.

In one British settlement, Papua, a part of New Guinea, the Australian Government is endeavouring to lead a Kanaka race along the path of modern progress. "Papua for the Papuans," is the keynote of the administration, and all kinds of devices are adopted to tempt the coloured man to industry. His Excellency, Colonel Murray, the Administrator of Papua, told me in London (where he was on leave) last year (1911) that he had some hopes that the cupidity of the Papuans would in time tempt them to some settled industry. They had a great liking for the White Man's adornments and tools, and, to gratify that liking, were showing some inclination for work. The effort is well meant, but probably vain. "Civilisation is impossible where the banana grows," declared an American philosopher: and the generalisation was sound. The banana tree provides food without tillage: and an organic law of this civilisation of ours is that man must be driven, by hunger and thirst and the desire for shelter, to plan, to organise, to make machines, to store.

Every nation in the Pacific has the same experience. In the Hawaiian Group, the American Power finds the native race helpless material for nation-making. The Hawaiian takes on a veneer of civilisation, but nothing can shake him from his habits of indolence. He adopts American clothes, lives in American houses, learns to eat pie and to enjoy ice-cream soda. He plays at the game of politics with voluble zeal. But he is still a Kanaka, and takes no real part in the progress of the flourishing territory of Hawaii. Americans do the work of administration. Imported Japanese, Chinese, Portuguese and others, are the coolies and the traders. The Hawaiian talks, basks in the sun, adorns himself with wreaths of odorous flowers, and occasionally declaims with the pathetic bleat of an enraged sheep at "American tyranny."

When White civilisation came to the South Pacific, the various islands held several millions of coloured peoples, very many of them enjoying an idyllically happy system of existence. To-day, 50,000 Maoris, beginning to hold their own in the islands of New Zealand, represent the sole hope of all those peoples to have any voice at all in the Pacific. Humanitarian effort may secure the survival for a time of other groups of islanders, but the ultimate prospects are not bright. Probably what is happening at Fiji, where the Fijian fades away in the face of a more strenuous coolie type imported from India, and at Hawaii, will happen everywhere in the South Pacific.

CHAPTER X

LATIN AMERICA

Latin America is the world's great example of race-mixture. Europeans and Indians have intermixed from Terra del Fuego to the northern boundary of Mexico, and the resultant race, with some differences due to climate, has general points of resemblance over all that vast territory. There is prompting to speculation as to the reasons why in Spanish and Portuguese America race mixture was the rule, in Anglo-Saxon America the exception. It was not the superior kindness of the Latin people which paved the way to confidence and inter-marriage. No one can doubt that, badly stained as are the records of the Anglo-Saxons in America, the records of the Latins are far, far worse. Yet the Latin, between intervals of massacre, prepared the nuptial couch, and a Latin-Indian race survives to-day whilst there is no Teutonic-Indian race.

Probably it is a superior sense of racial responsibility and racial superiority which has kept the Anglo-Saxon colonist from mingling his blood with that of the races he made subject to him. He shows a reproduction in a modern people of the old Hebraic spirit of elect nationality. In truth; there may be advanced some excuse for those fantastic theorists who write large volumes to prove that ten tribes were once lost from Israel and might have been found soon after in Britain. If there were no other circumstances on which to found the theory (which, I believe, has not the slightest historical basis), the translation of the Old Testament into the English language would amply serve. It is the one great successful translation of the world's literary history: it makes any other version of the Bible in a European language—including that pseudo-English one done at Douai—seem pallid and feeble; it rescues the Hebrew sentiment and the Hebrew poetry from out the morass of the dull Greek translation. And it does all this seemingly because the Elizabethan Englishman resembled in temperament, in outlook, in thought, the Chosen People of the time of David.

The Elizabethan Anglo-Saxon wandering out on the Empire trail treated with cruelty and contempt the Gentile races which he encountered. He has since learned to treat them with kindness and contempt. But he has never sunk the contempt, and the contempt saves him from any general practice of miscegenation. In ruling the blind heathen, more fussy peoples fail because they wish to set the heathen right: to induce the barbarian to become as they are. The Anglo-Saxon does not particularly wish to set the heathen right. He is right: that suffices. It is not possible for inferior races ever to be like him. It is wise, therefore, to let them wallow. So long as they give to him the proper reverence, he is satisfied. Thus the superb, imperturbable Anglo-Saxon holds aloof from inferior races: governs them coolly, on the whole justly; but never attempts to share their life. His plan is to enforce strictly from a subject people the one thing that he wants of them, and to leave the rest of their lives without interference. They may fill the interval with hoodoo rites, caste divisions or Mumbo-Jumbo worship, as they please. So long as such diversions have no seditious tendencies they are viewed, if not with approval, at least with tolerance. Indeed, if that be suitable to his purpose, the Anglo-Saxon governor of the heathen will subsidise the Dark Races' High Priest of Mumbo-Jumbo. Thus a favourite British remedy for the sorcerer, who is the great evil of the South Sea Islands, is not a crusade against sorcery, which would be very troublesome and rather useless, but to purchase over the chief sorcerers—who come very cheap when translated into English currency—and make them do their incantations on behalf of orderly government (insisting, by the way, on more faithful service than Balaam gave).

It is his race arrogance, equally with his robust common-sense, that makes the Anglo-Saxon the ideal coloniser and governor of Coloured Races: and there is no room for miscegenation in an ideal system. America, considered in its two sections, Latin America and Anglo-Saxon America, gives a good opportunity for comparison of colonising methods. To-day North of the 30th parallel the Republic of the United States shows as the greatest White nation of the world, greatest in population and material prosperity; and the young nation of Canada enters buoyantly upon the path of a big career. South of that parallel there are great populations, but they are poor in resources, and as a rule poorly governed, poorly educated. Some of the Latin-American races show promise—Chili and the Argentine Republic most of all,—yet none is comparable or ever likely to be comparable with the Republic of North America.

Yet before Columbus sailed from Europe the position was exactly reversed. North of the 30th parallel of northern latitude there was but a vagabond beginning of civilisation. South of that parallel two fine nations had built up polities comparable in many respects with those of the European peoples of to-day. What Peru and Mexico would have become under conditions of Anglo-Saxon conquest, it is, of course, impossible to say. But there is an obvious conclusion to be drawn from the fact that the Anglo-Saxon colonists found a wilderness and built up two great nations: the Latin colonists found two highly organised civilisations, and left a wilderness from which there now emerges a hope, faint and not yet certain, of a Latin-American Power.

The story of Peru is one of the great tragedies of history. The Peruvian Empire at the time of the Spanish invasion stretched along the Pacific Ocean over the territory which now comprises Ecuador, Peru, Bolivia, and Chili. Natural conditions along that coastal belt had been favourable to the growth of civilisation. A strip of land about twenty leagues wide runs along the coast, hemmed in by the Andes on one side, by the sea on the other. This strip of coast land is fed by a few scanty streams. Above, the steppes of the Sierra, of granite and porphyry, have their heights wrapped in eternal snows. Here was the call for work, which is the main essential of civilisation. The Peruvians constructed a system of canals and subterranean aqueducts, wrought with extraordinary skill by instruments and tools made of stone and copper (though iron was plentiful its use had not been learned). Thus they cultivated the waste places. In some respects their life conditions were similar to those of the Egyptians. Their agriculture was highly advanced and comprehensive. Their religion was sun-worship, and on it was based a highly organised theocracy. Tradition said that a son and daughter of the Sun, who were also man and wife, were sent by their father to teach the secrets of life to the Peruvians. These divinities were the first Incas.

The civil and military systems of the Peruvians were admirable in theory, though doomed to break down utterly under the savage test of the Spanish invasion. The Empire was divided into four parts; into each ran one of the great roads which diverged from Cuzco ("the navel"), the capital. The provinces were ruled by viceroys, assisted by councils; all magistrates and governors were selected from the nobility. By law, the Peruvian was forced to marry at a certain age. Sufficient land was allotted him to maintain himself and his wife, and an additional grant was made for each child. There was a yearly adjustment and renewal of land grants. Conditions of theocratic and despotic socialism marked most departments of civil life. In what may be called "foreign politics" the Incas pursued conquest by a Florentine policy of negotiation and intrigue. In dealing with neighbouring foes they acted so that when they at last came into the Peruvian Empire, they should have uncrippled resources and amicable sentiments. The Spaniards have described the Peruvians as "lazy, luxurious and sensual." It would have been equally correct to have said that they were contented, refined and amiable. Their very virtues made it impossible for them to defend themselves against the Spaniards.

The Spanish adventurers who were destined to destroy the elegant and happy civilisation of the Peruvians—a civilisation which had solved the problem of poverty, and gave to every citizen a comfortable existence—were children of Spain at her highest pitch of power and pride. Gold and his God were the two objects of worship of the Spaniard of that day, and his greed did no more to sully his wild courage with cruelty than his religion, which had been given a fierce and gloomy bent towards persecution by the struggles with the Moors.

In 1511 Vasco Nunez da Balboa was told in Mexico of a fabulously rich land where "gold was as cheap as iron." Balboa in the search for it achieved the fine feat of crossing from Central America the mountain rampart of the isthmus. Reaching the Pacific, he rushed into its waters crying, "I claim this unknown sea with all it contains for the King of Castile, and I will make good this claim against all who dare to gainsay it." There Balboa got clearer news of Peru, and pushed on to within about twenty leagues of the Gulf of St Michael. But the achievement of Peru was reserved for another man. In 1524 Francisco Pizarro set out upon the conquest of Peru. Pizarro had all the motives for wild adventure. An illegitimate child—his father a colonel of infantry, his mother of humble condition,—he had reached middle age without winning a fortune, yet without abating his ambition. He was ready for any desperate enterprise. After two unsuccessful attempts to reach Peru, the Spanish freebooter finally succeeded, leading a tiny force across the Andes to Caxamalco, where he encountered the Inca, who received the strangers peaceably. But no kindness could stave off the lust for gold and slaughter of the Spaniards. Because the Inca refused at a moment's notice to accept the Christian God, as explained to him by a Spanish friar, a holy war was declared against the Peruvians. The wretched people understood as little the treachery and the resolute cruelty of the Spaniards as their gunpowder and their horses. Paralysed by their virtues, they fell easy victims, as sheep to wolves.

A career of rapine and bloodshed led to the complete occupation of the country by the Spaniards, and the vassalage of the natives. Civil war amongst the conquerors, into which the natives were willy-nilly dragged, aggravated the horrors of this murder of a nation. The Spaniards looted and tortured the men, violated the women, and were so merciless as to carry on their war even against the natural resources of the country. They used to kill the llama or native sheep for the sake of its brains, which were considered a delicacy. Yet Pizarro, in his instructions from Spain, which secured to him the right of conquest and discovery in Peru, and various titles and privileges, was expressly enjoined "to observe all regulations for the good government and protection of the natives."

The fact that the Spaniards condescended to racial mixture with the Indians did nothing to heal the scars of such suffering. The half-breeds grew up with a hatred of Spain, and they had borrowed from their fathers some of their savagery. The mild Peruvian would have bred victims for generation after generation. The Spanish-Peruvian cross bred avengers. Early in the nineteenth century Spain was driven out of South America and a series of Latin-American Republics instituted.

In 1815 the Napoleonic wars having ended with the caging of the great soldier, Spain proposed to the Holy Alliance of European monarchs a joint European effort to restore her dominion over the revolted colonies in South America. But Napoleon had done his work too well to allow of any alliance, however "holy," to reassert the divine right of kings. Whilst he had been overthrowing the thrones of Europe, both in North and South America free nations had won recognition with the blood of their people. The United States, still nationally an infant, but sturdy withal, promulgated the Monroe doctrine as a veto on any European war of revenge against the South American Republics. Great Britain was more sympathetic to America than to the Holy Alliance. The momentarily re-established Kings and Emperors of Europe had therefore to hold their hand. It was a significant year, creating at once a free Latin America and a tradition that Latin America should look to Anglo-Saxon America for protection.

Passing north of the Isthmus of Panama, there come up for consideration another group of Latin-American States of which the racial history resembles closely that of South America. The little cluster of Central American States can hardly be taken seriously. Their ultimate fate will probably be that of Cuba—nominal independence under the close surveillance of the United States. But, farther north, Mexico claims more serious attention. Some time before Peru had received the blessings of civilisation from Pizarro, Mexico had reluctantly yielded her independence to Cortez, a Spanish leader whose task was much more severe than that of Pizarro. Whilst the mild Peruvians gave up without a struggle, the fierce Mexicans contested the issue with stubbornness and with a courage which was enterprising enough to allow them to seize the firearms of dead Spanish soldiers and use them against the invaders.

The original Aztec civilisation was warlike and Spartan. Extreme severity marked the penal codes. Intemperance, the consuming canker of Indian races, was severely penalised. There were several classes of slaves, the most unhappy being prisoners of war, who were often used as sacrificial victims to the gods. Sacrificed human beings were eaten at banquets attended by both sexes. The Aztecs were constantly at war with their neighbours, and needed no better pretext for a campaign than the need to capture sacrifices for their gods.

Grijalba was the first Spaniard to set foot on Mexico. He held a conference with an Aztec chief, and interchanged toys and trinkets for a rich treasure of jewels and gold. Cortez, the conqueror of Mexico, was sent to Mexico by Velasquez, conqueror of Cuba. He landed in Mexico with the avowed object of Christianising the natives, and considered himself a Soldier of the Cross. Like a good Crusader, he was ready to argue with the sword when words failed to convince. For some while he engaged in amicable relations with the Mexicans, exchanging worthless trifles for Mexican gold. But eventually various small wars led up to a three months' siege of the Aztec capital, which fell after a display of grand courage on the part of the Mexicans. Their civilisation, when at a point of high development, was then blotted out for ever.

It was in 1521 that the Spaniards first landed in Mexico. Their rule extended over three centuries. In 1813 Mexico first declared her independence, and in 1821 achieved the separation from Spain. The war of liberation had been fierce and sanguinary. It was succeeded by civil wars which threatened to tear to pieces the new nation. In 1822 an Empire was attempted. It ended with the assassination of the Emperor, Augustin de Yturbidi. A series of military dictatorships followed, until in 1857 a Republican constitution was promulgated. Because this constitution was strongly anti-clerical, it led to another series of wars.

Meanwhile greedy eyes were fixed upon the rich territories thus ravaged by civil strife. The United States to the north coveted the coastal provinces of California. Napoleon III. of France conceived the idea of reviving French influence on the American continent, and in 1864 helped to set up the second Empire of Mexico with the unhappy Maximilian at its head. Maximilian left Europe in the spring of 1864. After three years of civil war he was shot by the revolutionary commander. His rule had not commended itself to the Mexicans and was viewed with suspicion by the United States, which saw in it an attempt to revive European continental influences.

Then anarchy reigned for many years, until in 1876 the strong hands of Diaz, one of the great men of the century, took control. He did for the Mexican revolutionaries what Napoleon had done for the French Terrorists. But it was different material that he had to work upon. The Mexicans, their Aztec blood not much improved by an admixture of European, gave reluctant obedience to Diaz, and he was never able to lead them towards either a peaceful and stable democracy or a really progressive despotism. For more than a quarter of a century, however, he held power, nominally as the elected head of a Republic, really as the despotic centre of a tiny oligarchy. The country he ruled over, however, was not the old Spanish Mexico. There had been a steady process of absorption of territory by her powerful northern neighbour. Over 1,000,000 square miles, included in the rich Californian and Texas districts, had passed over by right of conquest or forced sale to the United States. The present area of Mexico is 767,000 square miles. So more than half of this portion of Spanish America has passed over to the Stars and Stripes.

The fall of Diaz in 1911 seemed to presage the acquirement by the United States of the rest of Mexico. There had been for some months rumours of an alliance between Mexico and Japan, which would have had an obviously unfriendly purpose towards the United States. The rumours were steadily denied. But many believed that they had some foundation, and that the mobilisation of United States troops on the Mexican frontier was not solely due to the desire to keep the frontier line secure from invasions by the Mexican revolutionaries. Whatever the real position, the tension relaxed when the abdication of Diaz allayed for a while the revolutionary disorders in Mexico. Now (1912) disorder again riots through Mexico, and again the authorities of the United States are anxiously considering whether intervention is not necessary.[5]

I am strongly of the opinion that by the time the Panama Canal has been opened for world shipping, the United States will have found some form of supervision over all Latin North America necessary: and that her diplomacy is now shaping also for the inclusion of Latin South America in an American Imperial system by adding to the present measure of diplomatic suzerainty which the Monroe doctrine represents a preferential tariff system. Before discussing that point, the actual strength of Latin America should be summarised. To-day the chief nations of Latin America—all of Spanish-Indian or of Portuguese-Indian origin—are:—

The Republic of Argentina, area 3,954,911 square miles; population, 6,489,000 (increasing largely by immigration from all parts of Europe); revenue, about £20,000,000 a year.

The Republic of Bolivia, area 605,400 square miles; population 2,049,000; revenue, about £1,300,000 a year.

The Republic of Brazil, area 3,218,991 square miles; population 21,461,000 (there is a great European immigration); revenue, about £18,000,000 a year.

The Republic of Chili, area 2474 square miles; population about 4,500,000; revenue about £1,400,000 a year.

The Republic of Ecuador, area 116,000 square miles; population about 1,400,000; revenue about £1,400,000.

The Republic of Uruguay, area 72,210 square miles; population 1,042,668; revenue about £5,000,000.

The Republic of Venezuela, area 393,870 square miles; revenue about £2,000,000.

The Republic of Paraguay, area 98,000 square miles; population about 650,000.

The Republic of Mexico, area 767,000 square miles; population about 14,000,000.

The total of populations is between 50,000,000 and 60,000,000.

These peoples have the possibility—but as yet only the possibility—of organising appreciable naval power, and are possessed now of a military power, not altogether contemptible, and equal to the task at most points of holding the land against a European or Asiatic invader, if that invader had to face the United States' naval power also. Presuming their peaceable acceptance of a plan to embrace them in the ambit of an American Imperial system—a system which would still leave them with their local liberties,— there is no doubt at all that they could add enormously to the strength of the United States. Presuming, on the other hand, a determined plan on their part to form among themselves a grand Federal League, and to aim at a Latin-American Empire, they might make some counterbalance to the power of the United States on the American continent and in the Pacific.

Neither contingency seems immediately likely. These Latin-American peoples have not yet shown any genius for self-government. They produce revolutionary heroes, but not statesmen. Among themselves they quarrel bitterly, and a Latin-American Confederation does not seem to be possible. On the other hand, Latin America is jealous of the United States: resents, whilst it accepts the benefits of, the Monroe doctrine, and would take as a danger signal any action hostile to the Mexican Republic which the Anglo-Celtic Republic should be forced to take. Any attempt on the part of the United States to "force the pace" in regard to Latin America would saddle her with half a dozen annoying wars.

What seems to be the aim of United States diplomacy, and what seems to be an attainable aim, is that very gradually the countries of South America will be brought closer to the northern Republic, coaxed by a system of reciprocity in trade which would offer them advantageous terms. Commercial union would thus pave the way to a closer political union. Such a development would be a very serious detriment to British trade interests, and to the British position in the Pacific. British export trade with Latin America is very considerable, amounting to some £60,000,000 worth a year. The two greatest contributors to the total are Brazil (£16,426,000 in 1910) and the Argentine Republic (£19,097,000 in 1910). Their communications with Great Britain will be left unchanged with the opening of the Panama Canal: and that event consequently will not strengthen American influence there. The same remark applies to trade with Mexico (£2,399,000 in 1910), with Columbia (£1,196,000), with Uruguay (£2,940,000). But trade with Peru (£1,315,000) and Chili (£5,479,000) will be affected by the canal bringing New York competition nearer.

There would, however, be a very serious position created for British trading interests if a proposal were carried out of an American preferential tariff system embracing the United States and Latin America. The total of British trade with Latin America (about £60,000,000) is nearly one-third of the total of British foreign trade (£183,986,000 in 1910), and is more than half the total British trade with British possessions. Moreover, it is almost exclusively in lines in which United States competition is already keenly felt. A tariff preference of any extent to the United States would drive British goods, to a large degree, out of the Latin-American market.

The position of Latin America in its effect on the dominance of the Pacific may be summed up as this: racial instability will probably prevent the Latin-American nations from federating and forming a great Power; the veto of the United States will prevent them from falling into the sphere of influence of any European Power; their jealousy and distrust of the United States, whether it be without or with reason, will stand in the way of their speedy absorption in an American Imperial system. But that absorption seems ultimately inevitable (though its form will leave their local independence intact). Its first step has been taken with the Monroe declaration; its second step is now being prepared with proposals for trade reciprocity.

CHAPTER XI

CANADA AND THE PACIFIC

The existence, side by side, of two races and two languages in Canada makes it a matter of some doubt as to what the future Canadian nation will be. The French race, so far proving more stubborn in its characteristics than the British race in Canada, has been the predominant influence up to recently, though its influence has sought the impossible aim of a French-Canadian nation rather than a Canadian nation. Thus it was at once a bulwark of national spirit and yet an obstacle to a genuinely progressive nationalism. Patriotic in its resistance to all external influences which threatened Canadian independence, it yet failed in its duty to promote an internal progress towards a homogeneous people.

Canada, it is perhaps needless to recall to mind, was originally a French colony. In the sixteenth century, when the British settlements in America were scattered along the Atlantic seaboard of what is now the United States, the French colonised in the valley of the Mississippi and along the course of the great river known as the St Lawrence. Their design of founding an Empire in America, a "New France," took the bold form of isolating the seaboard colonies of the British, and effectively occupying all of what is now the Middle-West of the United States, together with Canada and the country bordering on the Gulf of Mexico. It is not possible to imagine greater courage, more patient endurance, more strenuous enterprise, than was shown by the early founders of New France. If they did not achieve, they at least fully deserved an Empire.

French colonists in Canada occupied at first the province of Acadia, now known as Nova Scotia, and the province of Quebec on the River St Lawrence. Jacques Cartier, a sailor of St Malo, was the first explorer of the St Lawrence. Acadia was colonised in 1604 by an expedition from the Huguenot town of La Rochelle, under the command of Champlain, De Monts, and Poutrincourt. Then a tardy English rivalry was aroused. In 1614 the Governor of Virginia, Sir Thomas Dale, sent an expedition to Acadia, and took possession of the French fort. That was the first blow in a long struggle between English and French for supremacy in North America. In 1629, the date of Richelieu's supremacy in France, an incident of a somewhat irregular war between England and France was the capture, by David Kirk, an English Admiral, of Quebec, the newly-founded capital of "New France"; and the English Flag floated over Fort St Louis. But it was discovered that this capture had been effected after peace had been declared between the two European Powers, and, by the treaty of St Germain-en-Laye, Quebec was restored to France.

But the French colonies in America were still inconsiderable and were always threatened by the Red Indians, until Colbert, the great Minister of Louis XIV., made them a royal province, and, with Jean Baptiste Talon as Governor, Monseigneur Laval as Bishop, and the Marquis de Tracy as soldier, French Canada was organised under a system of theocratic despotism. The new régime was strictly paternal. The colonists were allowed no self-governing rights; a feudal system was set up, and the land divided into seignories, whose vassals were known as "habitants," a name which still survives. In all things the Governor and the Bishop exercised a sway. Wives were brought from France for the habitants, early marriages and large families encouraged, and religious orthodoxy carefully safeguarded.

The French Canada of to-day shows the enduring nature of the lessons which Talon and Laval then inculcated. With the growth of modern thought the feudal system has passed away, and the habitants are independent farmers instead of vassals to a seigneur. But in most other things they are the same as their forefathers of the seventeenth century. When Canada passed into the hands of the English, it had to be recognised that there was no hope of holding the country on any terms antagonistic to the habitants and their firmly fixed principles of life. In regard to religion, to education, to marriage and many other things, the old Roman Catholic ecclesiastical influence was preserved, and continues almost undiminished to this day.

The French-Canadian is a Frenchman of the era before the Revolution—a Frenchman without scepticism, and with a belief in large families. He is the Breton peasant of a century ago, who has come to a new land, increased and multiplied. He is devoutly attached to the Roman Catholic Church, and follows its guidance in all things.

A somewhat frigid and calculating "loyalty" to Great Britain; a deep sentimental attachment to France as "the Mother Country"; a rooted dislike to the United States, founded on the conviction that if Canada joined the great Republic he would lose his language and religious privileges—these are the elements which go to the making of the French-Canadian's national character.

Very jealously the French-Canadian priesthood preserves the ideas of the ancient order. Marriage of French-Canadians with Protestants, or even with Roman Catholics of other than French-Canadian blood, is discouraged. The education of the children—the numerous children of this race which counts a family not of respectable size until it has reached a dozen—is kept in the hands of the Church in schools where the French tongue alone is taught. Thus the French-Canadian influence, instead of permeating through the whole nation, aims at a people within a people. The aim cannot be realised; and already the theocratic idea, on which French-Canadian nationalism is largely based, shows signs of weakening. There are to be found French-Canadians who are confessedly "anti-clerical." That marks the beginning of the end. One may foresee in the near future the French-Canadian element merging in the general mass of the community to the great benefit of all—of the French-Canadian, who needs to be somewhat modernised; of the British-Canadian, who will be all the better for a mingling of a measure of the exalted idealism and spiritual strength of the French element; and of the nation at large, for a complete merging of the two races, French and British, in Canada would produce a people from which might be expected any degree of greatness.

Canada, facing to-day both the Atlantic and the Pacific, has the possibilities of greatness on either ocean, or indeed on both; I do not think it a wild forecast to say that ultimately her Pacific provinces may be greater than those bordering the Atlantic, and may draw to their port a large share of the trade of the Middle-West. Entering Canada by her Pacific gate, and passing through the coastal region over the Selkirks and Rockies to the prairie, one sees all the material for the making of a mighty nation. The coastal waters, and the rivers flowing into them, teem with fish, and here are the possibilities of a huge fishing population. At present those possibilities are, in the main, neglected, or allowed to be exploited by Asiatics. But a movement is already afoot to organise their control for the benefit of a British population. The coastal strip and the valleys running into the ranges are mild of climate and rich of soil. An agricultural population of 10,000,000 could here find sustenance, first levying toll on the great forests, and later growing grain and fruit. Within the ranges are great stores of minerals, from gold down to coal and iron. Everywhere are rushing rivers and rapids to provide electrical power. Fishermen, lumbermen, farmers, mountain graziers, miners, manufacturers—for all these there is golden opportunity. The rigours of the Eastern Canadian climate are missing: but there is no enervating heat. The somewhat old-fashioned traditions of the Eastern provinces are also missing, and the people facing the Pacific have the lusty confidence of youth.

At present the balance of political power in Canada is with the east. But each year sees it move farther west. The Pacific provinces count for more and more, partly from their increasing population, partly from their increasing influence over the prairie farmers and ranchers. The last General Election in Canada showed clearly this tendency. In every part of the nation there was a revulsion from the political ideals represented by Sir Wilfrid

Laurier: and that revulsion was most complete in the west, where as a movement it had had its birth.

It would be outside of the scope of this book to discuss the domestic politics of Canada, but the Canadian General Election of 1911 was so significant in its bearing on the future of the Pacific, that some reference to its issues and decisions is necessary. Sir Wilfrid Laurier up to 1911 had held the balance even between the British and the French elements in Canada without working for their amalgamation. His aim always was to pursue a programme of peaceful material development. With the ideals of British Imperialism he had but little real sympathy, and his conception of the duty of the Canadian nation was that it should grow prosperous quickly, push forward with its railways, and avoid entangling participation in matters outside the boundaries of Canada. He was not blind to the existence of the United States Monroe doctrine as a safeguard to Canadian territory against European invasion, and was not disposed to waste money on armaments which, to his mind, were unnecessary. The Canadian militia, which from the character of the people might have been the finest in the world, was allowed to become a mostly ornamental institution.[6]

At the Imperial Defence Conference in 1909, Sir Wilfrid refused to follow the lead of other self-governing Dominions in organising Fleet units, and the Canadian attitude was recorded officially as this:

"As regards Canada, it was recognised that while on naval strategical considerations a Fleet unit on the Pacific might in the future form an acceptable system of naval defence, Canada's double seaboard rendered the provision of such a Fleet unit unsuitable for the present. Two alternative plans, based upon annual expenditures respectively of £600,000 and £400,000,

* were considered, the former contemplating the provision of four cruisers of the 'Bristol' class, one cruiser of the 'Boadicea' class, and six destroyers of the improved 'River' class, the 'Boadicea' and destroyers to be placed on the Atlantic side and the 'Bristol' cruisers to be divided between the Atlantic and Pacific oceans." Yet it had been expected that Canada would at least have followed the Australian offer of a Pacific Fleet unit at a cost of £3,000,000 a year.

Sir Wilfrid Laurier's fall came when, in the natural development of his ideals of a peaceful and prosperous

Canada, sharing none of the responsibilities of the British Empire, but reckoning for her safety partly on its power, partly on the power of the United States, he proposed to enter into a Trade Reciprocity Treaty with the United States. The proposal was fiercely attacked, not only on the ground that it represented a partial surrender of Canadian nationalist ideals, but also on the charge that it was against the interests of British Imperialism. At the General Election which followed, Sir Wilfrid Laurier was decisively defeated. As an indication of the issues affecting the result, there is the anecdote that one of Sir Wilfrid Laurier's supporters ascribed the defeat chiefly to "the chap who wrote 'Rule Britannia.'"

Canada to-day faces the future with a purpose made clear, of cherishing her separate nationalism and her partnership in the British Empire. She will cultivate friendship with the United States, but she will not tolerate anything leading to absorption with the great Republic: and she will take a more active part in the defence of the Empire. The Laurier naval policy, which was to spend a little money uselessly, has been set aside, and Canada's share in the naval defence of the Empire is to be discussed afresh with the British Admiralty. A military reorganisation, of which the full details are not available yet, is also projected. It is known that the Defence Minister, Colonel Hughes, intends to strengthen the rural regiments, to establish local in addition to central armouries, and to stimulate recruiting by increasing the pay of the volunteers. He also contemplates a vigorous movement for the organisation of cadet corps throughout the whole country. It is a reasonable forecast that Canada, in the near future, will contribute to the defence of the Pacific a Fleet unit based on a "Dreadnought" cruiser and a militia force capable of holding her western coast against any but a most powerful invader. Her ultimate power in the Pacific can hardly be over-estimated. The wheat lands of the Middle-West and the cattle lands of the West will probably find an outlet west as well as east, when the growing industrial populations of Asia begin to come as customers into the world's food markets. Electric power developed in the great mountain ranges will make her also a great manufacturing nation: and she will suffer less in the future than in the past from the draining away of the most ambitious of her young men to the United States. The tide of migration has turned, and it is Canada now which draws away young blood from the Southern Republic.

CHAPTER XII

THE NAVIES OF THE PACIFIC

The present year (1912) is not a good one for an estimate of the naval forces of the Pacific. The Powers interested in the destiny of that ocean have but recently awakened to a sense of the importance of speedy naval preparation to avert, or to face with confidence, the struggle that they deem to be impending. By 1915 the naval forces in the Pacific will be vastly greater, and the opening of the Panama Canal will have materially altered the land frontiers of the ocean. A statement of the naval forces of to-day, to be useful, must be combined with a reasonable forecast of their strength in 1915.

Following, for convenience' sake, geographical order, the Pacific Powers have naval strength as follows:—

Russia.—Russia is spending some £12,000,000 a year on her navy, and is said to contemplate a force of sixteen "Dreadnoughts." Of these, four are now in hand, but the date of their completion is uncertain. At present Russia has no effective naval force in the Pacific, and but little elsewhere. The "Dreadnoughts" building—which are of a much-criticised type—are intended for use in European waters. The naval force of Russia in the Pacific for the present and the near future may be set down as negligible.

Japan.—Japan has two battleships of the "Dreadnought" class, the *Satsuma* and the *Aki*, in actual commission. By the time that this book is in print there should be two more in commission. They were launched in November 1910. According to modern methods of computation, a navy can be best judged by its "Dreadnought" strength, always presuming that the subsidiary vessels of a Fleet unit—cruisers, destroyers and submarines—are maintained in proper proportion of strength. Japan's naval programme aims at a combination of fortress ships ("Dreadnoughts"), speed ships (destroyers) and submarines, in practically the same proportion as that ruling in the British navy. The full programme, at first dated for completion in 1915, now in 1920, provides for twenty modern battleships, twenty modern armoured cruisers, one hundred destroyers, fifty submarines and various other boats. But it is likely that financial need will prevent that programme from being realised. For the current year the Japanese naval estimates amount to £8,800,000. At present the Japanese navy includes some two hundred ships, of which thirty-eight are practically useless. The possibly useful Fleet comprises seventeen battleships and battleship cruisers, nine armoured cruisers, fifty-seven destroyers, twelve submarines, four torpedo gunboats and forty-nine torpedo boats.

The Japanese navy is by far the strongest force in the Pacific, and is the only navy in the world with actual experience of up-to-date warfare, though its experience, recent as it is, has not tested the value of the "Dreadnought" type, which theoretically is the only effective type of battleship.

China.—At present China has twenty-six small boats in commission and five building. Her biggest fighting ship is a protected cruiser carrying six-inch guns. The naval strength of China is thus negligible.

The United States.—The United States cannot be considered as a serious Pacific naval Power until the Panama Canal has been completed.[7] Then under certain circumstances the greater part of her Fleet would be available for service in the Pacific. She spends some £26,000,000 yearly on her navy. She has at present four "Dreadnoughts" in commission, and by the time that this book is in print should have six. Her building programme provides for two new "Dreadnoughts," and the proper complement of smaller craft, each year.

In the last annual report on the United States navy (December 1911), Secretary Meyer stated that a total

of forty battleships, with a proportional number of other fighting and auxiliary vessels, was the least that would place the United States on a safe basis in its relations with the other world Powers, and "while at least two other Powers have more ambitious building plans, it is believed that if we maintain an efficient Fleet of the size mentioned, we shall be secure from attack, and our country will be free to work out its destiny in peace and without hindrance. The history of all times, including the present, shows the futility and danger of trusting to good-will and fair dealing, or even to the most solemnly binding treaties between nations, for the protection of a nation's sovereign rights and interests, and without doubt the time is remote when a comparatively unarmed and helpless nation may be reasonably safe from attack by ambitious well-armed Powers, especially in a commercial age such as the present."

Battleships 36 and 37, at the time in course of construction, were, he claimed, a distinct advance on any vessels in existence. These vessels would be oil-burners, and would carry no coal. They were to be of about the same size as the *Delaware*, but their machinery would weigh 3000 tons less, or a saving of 30 per cent., and the fire-room force would be reduced by 50 per cent. Concluding his report, Mr. Meyer said: "The Panama Canal is destined to become the most important strategical point in the Western Hemisphere, and makes a Caribbean base absolutely necessary. The best base is

Guantanamo Bay, Cuba, which Cuba has ceded to the United States for naval purposes. This base will enable the United States to control the Caribbean with all its lines of approach to the canal, and, with a torpedo base at Key West, will render the Gulf of Mexico immune from attack."

A new type of war machine, which is a combination of a submarine and a torpedo boat, is now being prepared for use in the United States navy. She is known as the "sub-surface torpedo boat." There is a submarine hull with machinery and torpedo armaments, and a surface hull—said to be unsinkable—divided into compartments. The whole vessel weighs six tons, can be carried on the deck of a battleship, travels eighteen knots an hour for a radius of two hundred miles, and needs a crew of two men. She carries a thousand pounds of gun-cotton. The sub-surface boat may be used as an ordinary torpedo boat, or she may be bodily directed at a hostile ship after her crew of two have left. It is estimated that the sub-surface boat will cost about £5000, all told, and it seems possible that it will be a serious weapon of naval warfare.

Great Britain.—Great Britain spent last year nearly £45,000,000 on her navy, which is the supreme naval force of the world. But its weight in a Pacific combat at present would be felt chiefly in regard to keeping the ring clear. No European Power hostile to Great Britain could send a Fleet into the Pacific. The United States could not despatch its Atlantic Fleet for service in the Pacific without a foreknowledge of benevolent neutrality on the part of Great Britain.

At the Imperial Defence Conference of 1909, it was decided to re-create the British Pacific Fleet, which, after the alliance with Japan, had been allowed to dwindle to insignificance. The future Pacific naval strength of Great Britain may be set down, estimating most conservatively, at a unit on the China station consisting of one "Dreadnought" cruiser, three swift unarmoured cruisers, six destroyers and three submarines. This would match the Australian unit of the same strength. But it is probable that a far greater strength will shortly be reached. It may be accepted as an axiom that the British—*i.e.* the Home Country—Fleet in Pacific waters will be at least kept up to the strength of the Australian unit. The future growth of that unit is indicated in the report on naval defence presented to the Commonwealth Government by Admiral Sir Reginald Henderson, a report which has been accepted in substance.

He proposes a completed Fleet to be composed as follows:—

8 Armoured Cruisers,
10 Protected Cruisers,
18 Destroyers,
12 Submarines,

3 Depôt Ships for Flotillas,
1 Fleet Repair Ship,
—
52.

This Fleet would, when fully manned, require a personnel of approximately 15,000 officers and men.

The Fleet to be divided into two divisions as follows:—

EASTERN DIVISION.

Class of Vessel.	Number.		
	In Full Commission.	With Reduced Crew.	Total.
Armoured cruiser	3	1	4
Protected cruiser	3	2	5
Torpedo-boat destroyer	8	4	12
Submarine	3	...	3
Depôt ship for torpedo-boat destroyers	2	...	2
Fleet repair ship	...	...	...
Total	19	7	26

WESTERN DIVISION.

Class of Vessel.	In Full Commission.	With Reduced Crew.	Total.
Armoured cruiser	3	1	4
Protected cruiser	3	2	5
Torpedo-boat destroyer	4	2	6
Submarine	9	...	9

Depôt ship for torpedo-boat destroyers	1	...	1
Fleet repair ship	1	...	1
Total	21	5	26
Grand total of both divisions	40	12	52

That would necessitate £3,000,000 a year expenditure for the first five years, rising gradually to £5,000,000 a year. To this the Australian Government is understood to be agreeable.

New Zealand does not propose to organise a naval force of her own, but will assist the British Admiralty with a subsidy. That subsidy is to be devoted to the use of the unit in China waters.

Canada's naval plans at present are not known. After the Imperial Defence Conference of 1909 Sir Wilfrid Laurier found both his instincts for frugality and for peace outraged by the forward policy favoured by other of the Dominions. He decided to sacrifice the former and not the latter, and embarked on a naval programme which, whilst it involved a good deal of expenditure, made it fairly certain that no Canadian warship would ever fire a shot in anger, since none would be completed until she had become hopelessly obsolete. His successor in office has stopped that naval programme. It is possible that the new administration will decide that Canada should contribute in some effective form to Imperial naval defence, and she may be responsible for a naval unit in the Pacific.

Latin America.—Brazil (whose interests, however, are in the Atlantic rather than the Pacific) has two modern battleships of the "Dreadnought" type, and one other building. Chili has at present no really modern warship, but projects two "Dreadnoughts" and up-to-date small craft. The existing Fleet consists of one battleship, two armoured cruisers, and four protected cruisers. The Republic of Argentine has at present several vessels practically obsolete, the most modern cruisers having been built in 1896. There are three battleships, four armoured cruisers, and three protected cruisers. A modern navy is projected with, as a nucleus, two 25,000-ton battleships of twenty-two knots, armed with twelve-inch guns. Mexico, Bolivia, Colombia, Ecuador, Paraguay, Uruguay, Venezuela, have no useful Fleets.

The following table will give as accurate a forecast as possible of naval strength in the Pacific in the immediate future:—

"DREADNOUGHT" TYPES IN 1912 AND 1915.

	1912	1915
British Empire	20	38
Germany	11	21
United States	8	14
Japan	4	8
Brazil	3	4
Argentine Republic	...	2
Chili	...	2

Note.—All the South American "Dreadnoughts" are open to some doubt, though Brazil has three vessels of the type actually in the water. Battleships and cruisers of the "Dreadnought" type are included in the above table. It has been computed on the presumption that there will be no change in the 1912 naval programmes. The United States, the British Empire and Japan, are stronger in battleships of the pre-Dreadnought period than is Germany. Russia is ignored, for she has no present intention of restoring her Pacific naval Power. Germany is included because of her future position as the second naval Power of the world, and her possible appearance in the Pacific as the ally of one or other of the Powers established there now.

The following additional table deals not merely with warships of the "Dreadnought" type, but with the effective tonnage, *i.e.* the tonnage of ships of all classes of the three greatest naval Powers:—

"EFFECTIVE TONNAGE" IN 1912 AND 1913-14.

	1912	1913-14
British Empire	1,896,149	2,324,579
United States	757,711	885,066
Germany	749,699	1,087,399

CHAPTER XIII

THE ARMIES OF THE PACIFIC

The military forces available for service in the Pacific are those (1) of Russia; (2) of China; (3) of Japan; (4) of the United States; (5) of the British Empire including India; (6) of the Latin-American peoples of Mexico and South America. The great armies of France, Germany, and Austro-Hungary can have no voice in the destinies of the Pacific Ocean unless indirectly, as, for instance, through Germany or Austria helping or hindering a Russian movement in the Far East by guaranteeing or threatening her European frontier.

The Russian army, though driven back by the forces of Japan during the recent war, still demands respectful consideration in any calculations as to the future of the Asian littoral of the Pacific Ocean. The Russians, as has been pointed out in a previous chapter, fought that campaign under many serious disadvantages. The Siberian railway gave them a very slender line of communication with their base. Now that railway is being duplicated, and in a future war would have at least double its old military capacity. The conditions of unrest at home in Russia during the war were so serious as almost to paralyse the executive government. Those conditions are not likely to be repeated, since Russia has now entered upon a fairly peaceful, if somewhat slow, progress towards constitutional reform. In a war on a land frontier for which the people were enthusiastic, the military power of Russia would be tremendous, though there was never any real foundation for the bogey of Russia as an all-powerful aggressive force.

The Russian army, based upon conditions of universal liability to service, can muster in the field for war some 4,000,000 of men. But considering the vast frontiers to be defended, and the great claims therefore made by garrison fortresses, it is not likely that more than 1,500,000 could be mobilised in any one district. It is reasonably possible to imagine a Russian army of a million men being brought to and maintained on the Pacific littoral: of an even greater army based on, say, Harbin. That would be a formidable force, especially if enrolled to fight for the White Races against an Asiatic peril: for then it would share the old military enthusiasm of the Cossacks.

There is nothing which will give the inquirer into national characteristics a better key to the Russian than a knowledge of the old Cossack organisation. It was formed, in the days of Russia's making as a nation, from the free spirits of the land, suffering on the one side from Turkish cruelty, on the other from the devastations of the Tartars. "Cossacks" meant simply "free men," and, at the outset, they were freebooters mainly, the Robin Hoods and Hereward the Wakes of Russia. But the patriotic work of resisting the Tartars and the Turks gave them a national aim, and in time they formed a military and religious organisation, unique in the history of European civilisation. From the village Cossacks—irregular volunteer troops, pursuing normally the life of villagers, but ready ever to take up arms against Tartar or Turkish bandits, or to become in turn themselves raiders of the enemy's caravans and villages—sprung up the Cossack Zaporojskoe, garrisoning the "Setch," a great military camp in the heart of the Cossack country. The Cossacks who joined the Setch devoted themselves wholly to military life. They had to swear to complete chastity, to abstinence whilst at war from alcohol, and to obedience to the Greek Church. The Cossack could leave the Setch if he were so inclined, but while he remained within its boundaries discipline was inexorable.

In the Setch there was neither organised training, nor compulsory drill, nor military manœuvres. With the exception of a few elected officers, there were, in time of peace, no social distinctions; but the bravest and the most experienced were treated with respect. For war a Cossack was elected to command each hundred men; his power was absolute. Several hundreds formed a regiment, with a colonel at its head, a temporary officer, elected for one campaign only. The organisation had some artillery and infantry, but its chief strength lay in its cavalry. It also built a Fleet of small boats with which it repeatedly raided the Turkish coast.

This military monastic order passed away with the closer organisation of the Russian nation. Despotic Czars could not tolerate a community so formidable in its virtues. Characteristically enough, it was Catherine the Great who dealt the final blow to the Cossack Setch. But the Cossack organisation and spirit, as well as the Cossack name, survive in the Russian army to-day, and the million or so men whom Russia could muster on the shores of the North Pacific might have some great say in the future destinies of the ocean.

The Japanese army of to-day, an army of veterans, must be credited, in calculating its value as a military engine, with the moral force of its record of victory. I confess to a belief in the superiority of the White Man, *qua* White Man over any Asiatic: and I am not inclined, therefore, to accept Japanese generalship and Japanese initiative at their Tokio valuation. But the 600,000 men whom Japan can put into the field, perfect in discipline, armed as to the infantry with a first-class rifle, a little deficient though they may be in artillery and cavalry, is a most formidable force, unassailable in Japan's home territory, not to be regarded lightly if called to a campaign on the Asiatic mainland. Since the war with Russia the Japanese army has been increased: the fact is evidence of the unslaked warlike enthusiasm of the people.

China will probably emerge from her present revolutionary troubles, whatever may be their result, with a seasoned army of great proportions. The actual military organisation of China at the time of the outbreak of the present revolt was somewhat nebulous. But an effort was being made to organise an Imperial army (on plans laid down in 1905) which would have numbered about 360,000 men trained on the Japanese model. Should the reformed China decide to follow in the footsteps of Japan as regards military organisation, the Chinese field force of the future would number some 2,500,000 men. It is already announced that the new Chinese Republic will adopt universal military training as part of its system of national reorganisation.

The United States, relying on a purely voluntary system for its military organisation, has, in the opinion of most critics, the framework of an army rather than an army. The peace strength of the United States regular army is about 100,000, and from these the Philippine garrison draws 13,000 men, and the Hawaiian garrison 1000 of all ranks. A partially trained militia numbers about 100,000 men. For the rest there are 16,000,000 of men of military age in the nation, but they are absolutely untrained. In case of a powerful enemy obtaining naval control of the Pacific, there is danger that the United States would suffer the ignominy of the occupation, for a time, of her Pacific coast.

British military forces available for the Pacific come under three headings:

> British garrisons in India and elsewhere in the Pacific.
>
> The citizen armies of Australia and New Zealand, and the militia forces of Canada.
>
> The Sepoy forces in India.

The British garrisons total some 80,000 men. They may be classed, without prejudice, among the best troops in the world, well trained and with some experience of warfare. But the majority of them are stationed in India, and few of them could be safely drawn from there in an emergency. The Sepoy troops number some 250,000, officered generally by British leaders. It is conceivable that a portion of them could be used outside of India against coloured races.

The citizen armies of Australia and New Zealand must be spoken of in the future tense: for their organisation has just begun, and it will be some five years before that organisation will be well under way. But so important is the bearing on Pacific problems of the training of some quarter of a million of citizen soldiers in the Australasian Dominions of the British Empire, that attention must be given here to a description of this army of the future.

Taking the Australian organisation as the model: The population of Australia in 1911 was about 4-1/2 millions, of whom there were, on the basis of the last census—

188,000 males of 14 years and under 18 years; and
295,000 males of 18 years and under 25 years.

Allowing for those living in districts too thinly populated to admit of training without excessive expenditure, or medically unfit for training, upon the figures at present available, it is estimated that Australia will have in training, when the scheme is in full operation, each year—

100,000 senior cadets; and
112,000 citizen soldiers.

The system will give in eight years' time a force of 126,000 trained men, and fully equipped. Every year afterwards will increase the reserve by 12,000 men. And if the training be extended into the country areas, the numbers may be increased by 40 per cent. Increase of population will bring, too, an increase of numbers, and my estimate of an eventual 200,000 for the Australian army and 50,000 for the New Zealand army is probably correct.

For the leading positions in this army there is provision to train a number of professional officers. The Military College of Australia is already in existence, and is organised on a basis of simplicity and efficiency which reflects the serious purpose of this democratic military organisation. It is not reserved for the children of the rich. It is not allowed to become intolerable to the children of the poor by the luxury of wealthy cadets. To quote from the official conditions:—

"The Military College of Australia is established to educate candidates for commissions in all arms of the Military Forces of the Commonwealth.

"Only candidates who intend to make the Military Forces their profession in life will be admitted as Cadets to the Military College. Parents or guardians are therefore not at liberty to withdraw their sons or wards at will.

"Cadets, in joining the Military College, shall be enlisted in the Permanent Military Forces for a term of twelve years. Service as a Cadet at the Military College shall be deemed service in the ranks of the Permanent Military Forces of the Commonwealth.

"No fees will be charged for equipment or instruction or maintenance of Cadets, and their travelling expenses within the Commonwealth between their parents' or guardians' residences and the College will be paid on first joining and on graduation.

"The following charges will be admitted against the public and credited to Cadets' accounts after they have joined:—

> "Outfit allowance—£30 on joining.
>
> "Daily allowance of five shillings and sixpence (5s. 6d.) to cover cost of uniform and clothing, books, instruments, messing, washing and other expenses.

"No Cadet will be permitted to receive money, or any other supplies from his parents or guardians, or any person whomsoever, without the sanction of the Commandant. A most rigid observance of this order is urged upon all parents and guardians, as its violation would make distinctions between Cadets, which it is particularly desired to prevent.

"No Cadet, when within the Federal Territory, or when absent on duty from College, or when in uniform, shall drink any spirituous or intoxicating liquor, or bring or cause the same to be brought within the College, or have the same in his room, tent, or otherwise in his possession.

"Gambling, lotteries, and raffles are strictly prohibited. They are serious offences, which will be severely punished.

"Smoking may be permitted during certain hours and in authorised places. The smoking of cigarettes is at all times prohibited. A Cadet found in possession of cigarettes is liable to punishment for disobedience of orders."

Canada has a militia force credited at present with a total strength of 55,000 men. Sir Wilfrid Laurier, who controlled the destinies of Canada for fifteen years up to 1911, was no military enthusiast and believed profoundly in a peaceful future for his country. In one respect, and in one respect only, Canada under his rule progressed in defence organisation: she had her own rifle factory turning out a rifle of Canadian design.

But a new spirit moves in Canada to-day in matters of Defence as in other things. I remember in 1909 speaking at Toronto in advocacy of a system of universal training for military service. Lieut.-Col. Wm. Hamilton Merritt, a Canadian militia officer who had learned enthusiasm for the idea of a "citizen army" on a visit to Switzerland, invited me to come up to Toronto from New York to speak on the Australian campaign for the universal training of citizens. The meeting was friendly but not particularly enthusiastic. My strongest recollection of it is that one Canadian paper most unjustifiably and absurdly twisted some words of mine advocating Canadian self-reliance into advice that Canada should arm "to attack the United States." But the outcome of the meeting was that a "Canadian

Patriotic League" was formed, and from it sprang the "Canadian Defence League, a non-political association to urge the importance to Canada of universal physical and naval or military training." For two years and more, in spite of the earnest efforts of Canadian enthusiasts, the movement languished. After the General Election of 1911, however, a quickening came to every department of Canadian life, and this particularly showed itself in matters of Defence. In November of that year, Colonel the Hon. S. Hughes, the Canadian Minister of Militia, called a conference of experts to consider the organisation of the militia. To that conference the Canadian Defence League was invited to send representatives, and their presence seemed to inspire the whole gathering with an enthusiasm for a universal service system. Summarising from a report sent to me by the Canadian Defence League: "Universal military training has at last become a live issue throughout the Dominion of Canada. It was the mainspring behind the whole machinery of the Militia Conference; almost every man present was in favour of it, but a few, if the question had come to vote, would have either refrained from voting or voted against it, because they were afraid of the possibility of being misunderstood by the public at large. The cavalry section made no recommendation, and the infantry section discussed it, while the artillery, which is always in the front, was strongly in favour of it. Colonel Logie of Hamilton moved and Colonel Fotheringham of Toronto seconded a resolution recommending the adoption of the Australian system in Canada. This motion was with a view to placing the conference on record; but the Minister, in his wisdom, held the resolution in abeyance, and it did not come to a vote. But in the closing hours of the conference Senator Power of Nova Scotia positively and definitely advocated universal military training for the whole of Canada."

A universal service system in Canada would provide a citizen army of—probably—250,000 men of the finest type: and the effect of this force on Pacific issues would be equal to that of the combined armies of Australia and New Zealand.

The military strength of Latin America (the South American Republics and Mexico) it is difficult to estimate accurately. In almost all cases the constitution of the Republics provides for "universal service" but fails to provide for universal training for service. Under modern conditions of warfare, it is useless to enact that men shall serve unless the necessary sacrifices of money and leisure are made to train them to serve. Raw levies could be made of some use almost immediately in a past epoch of warfare, when the soldier with his "Brown Bess" musket had the injunction from the drill sergeant to "wait until he could see the whites of the eyes" of his enemy and then to fire. That needed stolid nerves mainly, and but little training. In these days raw levies would be worse than useless, of no value in battles, a burden on the commissariat and hospital services between battles. The Latin-American armies must be judged in the light of that fact. Apart from that caution, the numbers are imposing enough.

Mexico has an army organisation providing for 30,000 men on a peace footing and 84,000 men on a war footing. The Argentine army on a peace footing is about 18,000 strong; on a war footing about 120,000 strong, exclusive of the National Guard and Territorial troops (forming a second line). In the Republic of Bolivia the peace footing of the army is 2500: the probable war footing 30,000. The Republic of Brazil has a universal service system. The peace strength of the army is 29,000 (to which may be added a gendarmerie of 20,000). On the outbreak of war there could be mobilised, it is claimed, five divisions totalling, say, 60,000 men. Chili has, on a peace footing, about 10,000 men; on a war footing 50,000, exclusive of the reserves (about 34,000). Colombia makes every man liable to service, but the training is not regular. Possibly 10,000 men could be mobilised in time of war. Ecuador maintains a permanent force of about 5000 men, and claims that it could mobilise 90,000 in case of war. Paraguay has a permanent force of 2500 men and a National Guard available for service in case of war.

The South American has proved himself, on occasions, a good and plucky fighter. But I doubt whether his military forces can be seriously considered as a factor in the fate of the Pacific, except in the matter of defending his own territory from invasion. The only armies that count greatly to-day in the Pacific are those of Japan, Russia, and Great Britain, in that order, with China and the United States as potential rather than actual military forces.

CHAPTER XIV

TREATIES IN THE PACIFIC

There is one actual alliance between two Pacific Powers, Great Britain and Japan: an *entente* between Great Britain and Russia: and an instinct towards friendliness between Great Britain and the United States. There are several other possible combinations affecting the ocean in the future. But no Power of the Triple Alliance, nor yet France, can be considered a factor in the Pacific except in so far as it may help or hinder a Power already established there. Germany, for instance, might enter the Pacific as an ally of Japan or the United States; but she could not without an alliance bring naval or military force there unless Great Britain had first been humbled in a European war.

To the alliance between Great Britain and Japan not very much importance can be ascribed since its revision in 1911. It threatens to die now of inanition, as it becomes clear that British aims and Japanese aims in the Pacific do not move towards a common end. The first British-Japanese treaty, signed on January 30, 1902, had for its main provisions—

"The Governments of Great Britain and Japan, actuated solely by a desire to maintain the *status quo* and general peace in the extreme East, being moreover specially interested in maintaining the independence and territorial integrity of the Empire of China and the Empire of Corea, and in securing equal opportunities in those countries for the commerce and industry of all nations, hereby agree as follows:—

"The High Contracting Parties, having mutually recognised the independence of China and of Corea, declare themselves to be entirely uninfluenced by any aggressive tendencies in either country. Having in view, however, their special interests, of which those of Great Britain relate principally to China, while Japan, in addition to the interests which she possesses in China, is interested in a peculiar degree politically, as well as commercially and industrially, in Corea, the High Contracting Parties recognise that it will be admissible for either of them to take such measures as may be indispensable in order to safeguard those interests if threatened either by the aggressive action of any other Power, or by disturbances arising in China or Corea, and necessitating the intervention of either of the High Contracting Parties for the protection of the lives and property of its subjects.

"If either Great Britain or Japan, in the defence of their respective interests as above described, should become involved in war with another Power, the other High Contracting Party will maintain a strict neutrality, and use its efforts to prevent other Powers from joining in hostilities against its ally.

"If in the above event any other Power or Powers should join in hostilities against that ally, the other High Contracting Party will come to its assistance and will conduct the war in common, and make peace in mutual agreement with it.

"The High Contracting Parties agree that neither of them will, without consulting the other, enter into separate arrangements with another Power to the prejudice of the interests above described.

"Whenever, in the opinion of either Great Britain or Japan, the above-mentioned interests are in jeopardy, the two Governments will communicate with one another fully and frankly."

A letter covering the treaty, addressed by the Marquess of Lansdowne to the British Minister at Tokio, Sir C. Macdonald, explained the fact that there was to be no disturbance of Chinese or Corean territory: "We have each of us desired that the integrity and independence of the Chinese Empire should be preserved, that there should be no disturbance of the territorial *status quo* either in China or in the adjoining regions, that all nations should, within those regions, as well as within the limits of the Chinese Empire, be afforded equal opportunities for the development of their commerce and industry, and that peace should not only be restored, but should, for the future, be maintained. We have thought it desirable to record in the preamble of that instrument the main objects of our common policy in the Far East to which I have already referred, and in the first Article we join in entirely disclaiming any aggressive tendencies either in China or Corea."

But that stipulation did nothing to safeguard Corea's independence, which was soon sacrificed to Japanese ambition. There was a widespread feeling of uneasiness in the British Dominions in the Pacific when this treaty was announced. At the time Canada was having serious trouble on her Pacific Coast with Japanese immigrants, and the Canadian Pacific provinces were anxious to prohibit absolutely the entry of more Japanese to their territory.[8] Australia in 1901 had made the first great deed of her new national organisation a law practically prohibiting all coloured immigration, and making the entry of Japanese colonists impossible. The Act certainly veiled its hostility to the Asiatic races by a subterfuge. It was not stated in so many words that black skin, brown skin, and yellow skin were prohibited from entry, but an educational standard was set up which might be applied to any immigrant, but needed to be applied to none. In practice it is never applied to the decent White but always to the coloured man: and its application is such that the coloured man can never be sure that his standard of

education will be sufficiently high to satisfy the fastidious sense of culture of an Australian Customs officer. He may be a learned Baboo, B.A. of Oxford, and Barrister of the Inner Temple, and yet fail to pass the Australian Education Test, for the ordeal is to take dictation in any European language, not necessarily English, but perhaps Russian or modern Greek. New Zealand, without going so far by her legislation, shows an equal repugnance to any form of Asiatic immigration.

The "official" view of the British Alliance with Japan, advocated with some energy, was that it was a benefit to the White Dominions in the Pacific, for it made them secure against the one aggressive Asiatic Power. But nevertheless the policy of making the wolf a guardian of the sheep-fold was questioned in many quarters. The question was asked: "Presuming a Pacific war in which the United States was the enemy of Japan?" The answer in the minds of many, in Australia at any rate, and probably also in Canada and New Zealand, was that in such event the sympathy, if not the active support, of the British Dominions in the Pacific would be with the United States, whether Great Britain kept to her Treaty or not. It was recognised, however, as almost unthinkable that Great Britain would go to war by the side of Japan against the American Republic.

Great Britain is very sensitive to the opinions of her Dominions in these days of the industrious promulgation of Imperialist sentiment in Great Britain: and a Canadian or an Australian voter—though he has no vote for the House of Commons—has far more influence on the destinies of the Empire than his British compeer. The overseas objection to the Treaty with Japan had its full effect in the British Cabinet, and that effect was seen in subsequent modifications of the Treaty.

On August 12, 1905, the British-Japanese Treaty was renewed, and the chief articles of the new treaty were:—

"The Governments of Great Britain and Japan, being desirous of replacing the agreement concluded between them on the 30th January, 1902, by fresh stipulations, have agreed upon the following articles, which have for their object—

"(a) The consolidation and maintenance of the general peace in the regions of Eastern Asia and of India;

"(b) The preservation of the common interests of all Powers in China by insuring the independence and integrity of the Chinese Empire and the principle of equal opportunities for the commerce and industry of all nations in China;

"(c) The maintenance of the territorial rights of the High Contracting Parties in the regions of Eastern Asia and of India, and the defence of their special interests in the said regions:—

"It is agreed that whenever, in the opinion of either Great Britain or Japan, any of the rights and interests referred to in the preamble of this Agreement are in jeopardy, the two Governments will communicate with one another fully and frankly, and will consider in common the measures which should be taken to safeguard those menaced rights or interests.

"If by reason of unprovoked attack or aggressive action, wherever arising, on the part of any other Power or Powers, either Contracting Party should be involved in war in defence of its territorial rights or special interests mentioned in the preamble of this Agreement, the other Contracting Party will at once come to the assistance of its ally, and will conduct the war in common, and make peace in mutual agreement with it.

"Japan possessing paramount political, military, and economic interests in Corea, Great Britain recognises the right of Japan to take such measures of guidance, control, and protection in Corea as she may deem proper and necessary to safeguard and advance those interests, provided always that such measures are not contrary to the principle of equal opportunities for the commerce and industry of all nations.

"Great Britain having a special interest in all that concerns the security of the Indian frontier, Japan recognises her right to take such measures in the proximity of that frontier as she may find necessary for safeguarding her Indian possessions.

"The High Contracting Parties agree that neither of them will, without consulting the other, enter into separate arrangements with another Power to the prejudice of the objects described in the preamble of this Agreement.

"The conditions under which armed assistance shall be afforded by either Power to the other in the circumstances mentioned in the present Agreement, and the means by which such assistance is to be made available, will be arranged by the naval and military authorities of the Contracting Parties, who will from time to time consult one another fully and freely upon all questions of mutual interest.

"The present Agreement shall, subject to the provisions of Article VI., come into effect immediately after the date of its signature, and remain in force for ten years from that date."

It will be noted that there is, as regards the general responsibility under the Treaty, some watering down. One Power is bound to come to the help of the other Power only by reason of "unprovoked attack or aggressive action" on the part of another Power. The fiction of preserving the independence of Corea is abandoned.

On April 3, 1911, a Treaty of Commerce and Navigation was entered into between Great Britain and Japan. The Japanese Government had revised its tariff in such a way as to prejudice seriously foreign trade. It was announced in Japan that certain nations would have the benefit of "most-favoured nation" rates under the new tariff, but that Great Britain would not have that benefit, since, being a Free Trade country, she was able to give no con*cessions in return. Then the diplomatic Treaty of 1905 was used by the British Government as an argument for securing more favoured treatment for British merchants. If the Trade Treaty of 1911 is closely studied, it will be found that the trade advantages given to Japan by Great Britain, in return for some real concessions on the part of Japan to Great Britain, are wholly illusory. It is difficult to see how they could have been otherwise, since a Free Trade country can give nothing better than Free Trade to another country. But Great Britain, a good deal out of conceit at this time with the diplomatic value of the Treaty of 1905, did not hesitate to use it as a means of securing some trade benefits. The effect on Japanese public opinion was not favourable. But the diplomatic position had so changed that that was not considered a serious circumstance in Great Britain.

Two articles of the British-Japanese Trade Treaty of 1911 should be quoted to show the mutual acceptance by the two Powers of the independent right of the British overseas Dominions to restrict or prohibit Japanese immigration:

"The subjects of each of the High Contracting Parties shall have full liberty to enter, travel and reside in the territories of the other, and, conforming themselves to the laws of the country,

"They shall in all that relates to travel and residence be placed in all respects on the same footing as native subjects.

"They shall have the right, equally with native subjects, to carry on their commerce and manufacture, and to trade in all kinds of merchandise of lawful commerce, either in person or by agents, singly or in partnerships with foreigners or native subjects.

"They shall in all that relates to the pursuit of their industries, callings, professions, and educational studies be placed in all respects on the same footing as the subjects or citizens of the most favoured nation."

But Article 26 makes this reservation:

"The stipulations of the present Treaty shall not be applicable to any of His Britannic Majesty's Dominions, Colonies, Possessions, or Protectorates beyond the seas, unless notice of adhesion shall have been given on behalf of any such Dominion, Colony, Possession, or Protectorate by His Britannic Majesty's Representative at Tokio before the expiration of two years from the date of the exchange of the ratifications of the present Treaty."

A few weeks after the conclusion of this Trade Treaty the British-Japanese Alliance was renewed on terms which practically "draw its sting" and abolish the contingency of a British-Japanese war against the United States, or against any Power with which Great Britain makes an Arbitration Treaty. The preamble of the British-Japanese Treaty now reads:

"The Government of Great Britain and the Government of Japan, having in view the important changes which have taken place in the situation since the conclusion of the Anglo-Japanese Agreement of the 12th August, 1905, and believing that a revision of that Agreement responding to such changes would contribute to the general stability and repose, have agreed upon the following stipulations to replace the Agreement above mentioned, such stipulations having the same object as the said Agreement, namely:

"(a) The consolidation and maintenance of the general peace in the regions of Eastern Asia and of India.

"(b) The preservation of the common interests of all Powers in China by insuring the independence and integrity of the Chinese Empire, and the principle of equal opportunities for the commerce and industry of all nations in China.

"(c) The maintenance of the territorial rights of the High Contracting Parties in the regions of Eastern Asia and of India and the defence of their special interests in the said regions."

The chief clauses are:

"If, by reason of unprovoked attack or aggressive action wherever arising on the part of any Power or Powers, either High Contracting Party should be involved in war in defence of its territorial rights or special interests mentioned in the preamble of this Agreement, the other High Contracting Party will at once come to the assistance of its ally and will conduct the war in common and make peace in mutual agreement with it.

"The High Contracting Parties agree that neither of them will, without consulting the other, enter into separate arrangements with another Power to the prejudice of the objects described in the preamble of this Agreement.

"Should either High Contracting Party conclude a Treaty of General Arbitration with a third Power, it is agreed that nothing in this Agreement shall entail upon such Contracting Party an obligation to go to war with the Power with whom such Treaty of Arbitration is in force.

"The present Agreement shall come into effect immediately after the date of its signature, and remain in force for ten years from that date."

It will be recognised that there is very little left now of the very thorough Treaty of 1902. It does not suit Japanese foreign policy that this fact should be accentuated, and public opinion in that country has been generally muzzled. Nevertheless, some candid opinions on the subject have been published in the Japanese press. Thus the Osaka *Mainichi* last January, discussing evidently a Japanese disappointment at the failure of Great Britain to join Japan in some move against Russia, claimed that "for all practical purposes, the Anglo-Japanese Alliance ended with its revision last July." In the opinion of the *Mainichi*, "the Alliance no longer furnishes any guarantee for the preservation of Chinese integrity. So far from Japan and Great Britain taking, as the terms of the Alliance provide, joint action to protect the rights and interests of the two nations when the same are threatened, no measures have been taken at all." According to the *Mainichi*, "England is no longer faithful to the principle of the Alliance as regards the territorial integrity of China, and it is even rumoured that she has intentions on Tibet, similar to those of Russia in Mongolia. Consequently it is a matter of supreme importance to know whether the Alliance is to be considered as still alive or not, and the Japanese Government would do well to make some explicit declaration on the subject."

This view was supported by the Tokio *Nichi-Nichi*, which wrote: "For a long time now the feeling between Great Britain and Japan has been undergoing a change. There is no concealing the fact that it is no longer what it was before the Russo-Japanese War. At the time of the Tariff the friendly relations were only maintained by concessions from the side of the Japanese. The revision of the terms of the Alliance has reduced it from a real value to this country to a merely nominal value. The friendship which has been steadily growing between Great Britain and Russia is something to be watched. The action of Great Britain in the China trouble has not been true to the Alliance. The tacit consent given to Russian action in Mongolia is a violation of the integrity of China, and on top of it we are informed that Great Britain at the right moment will adopt similar steps in Tibet."

The British-Japanese Treaty, for as much as it stands for, is the only definite treaty affecting big issues in the Pacific to-day. To attempt to discuss all possible treaties and combinations in the Pacific would be, of course, impossible. But some notice must be given of the recent remarkable hint of the possibilities of an "understanding" between Germany and the United States on Pacific questions. In February Mr Knox, the United States Secretary of State for Foreign Affairs, communicated in a formal Note to Germany some views on Pacific questions. Commenting on this, the *New York Sun*, whose correspondent at Washington is a great deal in the confidence of the Government, commented: "The significance of Mr Knox's Note as a warning will, it is thought, be clearly seen by the other Powers. The fact that the writing and publication of Mr Knox's Note are the result of an understanding between Germany and the United States will greatly add to the force of the document. The other Powers, according to the Washington view, will hesitate long before embarking upon the policy of advancing their special interests by taking advantage of China's distress when Germany and the United States are standing together before the world in opposition to any such move."

An "understanding" between Germany and the United States to act together on the Asiatic side of the Pacific littoral would have its strategic importance in the fact that German power in the Atlantic would help to lessen certain risks consequent upon the United States concentrating her naval forces in the Pacific.

Another reasonably possible combination should be noted. As one of three partners in the Triple Entente, Great Britain has an understanding with Russia, which might possibly affect one day the position in the Pacific. It is a fact rumoured among European diplomats that France, with the idea of maintaining the Triple Entente as a basis of future world-action, has urged Russia to build a Pacific Fleet, abandoning naval expansion in the Baltic and the Black Sea. With a strong Pacific Fleet Russia would certainly be a much more valuable friend to France and to Great Britain than at present. But that is "in the air." The actual position is that Great Britain and Russia are on such excellent terms that they can fish amicably together to-day in the very disturbed waters of Persia, and are possible future partners in the Pacific.

Those who consider a British-Russian alliance as impossible, forget the history of centuries and remember only that of a generation. Anciently the Russian and the Englishman were the best of friends, and Russian aid was often of very material use to Great Britain. It was in the eleventh century that King Canute established English naval power in the Baltic, and thus opened up a great trade with the Russian town of Novgorod. He helped the young Russian nation much in so doing. After Canute's death this trade with Russia languished for five centuries. But in the sixteenth century it was revived, and some centuries later it was said of this revival: "The discovery of a maritime intercourse with the Great Empire of Russia, and the consequent extension of commerce and navigation, is justly regarded by historians as the first dawn of the wealth and naval preponderance of England." Some indeed hold that the great exploits of the Elizabethan era of British seamanship would not have been possible without the maritime supplies—cordage, canvas, tallow, spars and salt beef—obtained from Russia.

The benefits of the friendship were not all on one side. In the seventeenth century England helped Russia with arms, supplies and troops against the Poles. In 1747 England paid Russia to obtain an army of 37,000 troops which was employed in Holland. Later it was agreed that Russia was to keep ready, on the frontiers of Livonia, an army of 47,000 troops beside forty galleys to be used in the defence of Hanover, for England, if needed. At a later date Catherine the Great of Russia was appealed to for 20,000 troops for service against the revolted American colonies, an appeal which she very wisely rejected. In the wars against Napoleon, Great Britain and Russia were joint chiefs of the European coalition, and a Russian Fleet was stationed in British waters doing good service at the time of the Mutiny of the Nore. A British-Russian understanding, in short, has been the rule rather than the exception in European politics since the fifteenth century.

An instinct of friendliness between Great Britain and the United States, though expressed in no formal bonds, is yet a great force in the Pacific. There has been at least one occasion on which an American force in the Pacific has gone to the help of a British naval force engaging an Asiatic enemy. There are various more or less authentic stories showing the instinct of the armed forces of both nations to fraternise. Sometimes it is the American, sometimes the British sailor who is accused of breaking international law in his bias for the men of his own speech and race. It would not be wise to record incidents, which were irregular if they ever happened, and which, therefore, had best be forgotten. But the fact of the American man-of-war's-men in Apia Harbour, Samoa, finding time during their own rush to destruction at the hands of a hurricane to cheer a British warship steaming out to safety, is authentic, and can be cited without any harm as one instance of the instinctive friendship of the two peoples in the Pacific of common blood and common language.

CHAPTER XV

THE PANAMA CANAL

The poetry that is latent in modern science, still awaiting its singer, shows in the story of the Panama Canal. Nature fought the great French engineer, de Lesseps, on that narrow peninsula, and conquered him. His project for uniting the waterways of the Pacific and the Atlantic was defeated. But not by hills or distances. Nature's chief means of resistance to science was the mobilising of her armies of subtle poisoners. The microbes of malaria, yellow fever, of other diseases of the tropical marshes, fell upon the canal workers. The mortality was frightful. Coolie workers, according to one calculation, had a year's probability of life when they took to work on the canal. The superintendents and engineers of the White Race went to their tasks as soldiers go to a forlorn hope. Finally the forces of disease conquered. The French project for cutting a canal through the isthmus of Panama was abandoned, having ruined the majority of those who had subscribed to its funds, having killed the majority of those who had given to it of their labour.

The United States having decided to take over the responsibility for a task of such advantage to the world's civilisation, gave to it at the outset the benefit of a scientific consideration touched with imagination. There were hills to be levelled, ditches to be dug, water-courses to be tamed, locks to be built. All that was clear enough. But how to secure the safety of the workers? Nature's defenders, though fed fat with victory, were still eager, relentless for new victims. Science said that to build a canal wholesome working conditions must be created: yellow fever and malaria abolished. Science also told how. The massacre of the mosquitoes of the isthmus was the first task in canal-building.

The mosquitoes, the disseminators of the deadly tropical diseases, were attacked in their breeding grounds, and their larvæ easily destroyed by putting a film of oil over the surface of the shallow waters in which they lived. The oil smothered the life in the larvæ, and they perished before they had fully developed. The insect fortunately has no great range of flight. Its life is short, and it cannot pass far from its birthplace. Herodotus tells how Egyptians avoided mosquitoes by sleeping in high towers. The natives of Papua escape them by building their huts in the forks of great trees. If the mosquitoes are effectively exterminated within a certain area, there is certainty of future immunity from them within that area if the marshes, the pools—the stagnant waters generally on its boundaries—are thereafter guarded during the hatching season against the chance of mosquito larvæ coming to winged life. At Suez scientists had found this all out. Science conquered the mosquito in Panama as it had been conquered elsewhere, and the entrenchments of Nature crumbled away. Henceforth it was a matter of rock-cutters, steam shovels and explosives, the A B C of modern knowledge. But the mosquito put up a stubborn fight. Driven out of the marshes, it found a refuge in the cisterns of houses, even in the holy-water founts of churches. Every bit of stagnant water within the isthmus area had to be protected against the chance of mosquitoes coming to life before the campaign was successful. To-day the isthmus of Panama is by no means unhealthy, and the work of canal-cutting progresses so well that Mr President Taft was able to announce recently the probability of it being opened two years before the due date. That brings the canal as a realised fact right into the present.

Some few facts regarding this engineering work. It will cost about £70,000,000. The total length of the canal to be made from sea to sea is 50-1/2 miles, with a maximum width on the bottom of 1000 feet. The land excavation is 40-1/2 miles of cutting through rock, sand and clay, leaving 10 miles of channel to be deepened to reach the sea at either end. Some of the other construction dimensions are these:—

Locks, usable length 1,000 feet.
Locks, usable width 110 feet.
Gatun Lake, area 164 square miles.
Gatun Lake, channel depth 84 to 45 feet.
Excavation, estimated total 174,666,594 cubic yards.
Concrete, total estimated for canal 5,000,000 cubic yards.

The Gatun is the greatest rock and earth-fill dam ever attempted. Forming Gatun Lake by impounding the waters of the Chagres and other streams, it will be nearly 1-1/2 miles long, nearly 1/2 mile wide at its base, about 400 feet wide at the water surface, about 100 feet wide at the top. Its crest, as planned, will be at an elevation of 115 feet above mean sea-level, or 30 feet above the normal level of the lake. The interior of the dam is being formed of a natural mixture of sand and clay placed between two large masses of rock, and miscellaneous material obtained from steam-shovel excavation at various points along the canal.

Gatun Lake will cover an area of 164 square miles, with a depth in the ship channel varying from 85 to 45 feet. The necessity for this artificial lake is because of the rugged hills of Panama. A sea-level canal would have been a financial impossibility. By a lock system lifting vessels up to Gatun Lake (a height of 85 feet), an immense amount of excavation was saved. Incidentally the alarm was allayed of that ingenious speculator who foretold that the Gulf Stream would take a new path through the Panama Canal and desert the West Coast of Europe, on the climate of which it has so profound an influence. When the canal was opened England was to revert to her "natural climate"—that of Labrador! But since the canal will not be a sea-level one, it cannot of course have the slightest effect on ocean currents. The amount of Pacific and Atlantic water which will be mutually exchanged by its agency each year will be insignificant.

The Panama Canal, when opened, will be exclusively United States property; it will be fortified and defended by the United States army and navy: and it will probably in time of peace be used to help United States trade, and in time of war to help the United States arms. All those conclusions are natural, since the United States has found the money for the work, and claims under the Monroe doctrine an exclusive hegemony of the American continent south of the Canadian border. But originally it was thought that the canal would be, in a sense, an international one. Later the idea was entertained, and actually embodied, in a treaty between Great Britain and the United States that whilst "the United States should have the exclusive right of providing for the regulation and management of the canal," it should not be fortified. But the Treaty of 1902 between Great Britain and the United States abrogated that, and provided for the "neutralisation" of the canal. It was stipulated that "the United States adopts, as the basis of the neutralisation of such ship canal, the following rules, substantially as embodied in the Convention of Constantinople, signed the 28th October 1888, for the free navigation of the Suez Canal." The Rules provide that the canal shall be open to the vessels of commerce and war of all nations on terms of equality, so that there shall be no discrimination against any nation or its citizens or subjects in respect to conditions or charges.

Rule 2 states: "The canal shall never be blockaded, nor shall any right of war be exercised, nor any act of hostility be committed within it. The United States, however, shall be at liberty to maintain such military police along the canal as may be necessary to protect it against lawlessness and disorder." The third rule prohibits vessels of war of a belligerent from revictualling or taking on stores in the canal except so far as may be strictly necessary. Under Rule 4 belligerents may not embark or disembark troops, munitions of war, or warlike materials, except in case of accidental hindrance in transit, "and in that case the transit shall be resumed with all possible despatch. Waters adjacent to the canal within three marine miles of either end are considered as part of the canal. Vessels of war of a belligerent are not permitted to remain in those waters longer than twenty-four hours, except in case of distress." The last rule makes the plant, establishments, buildings, and the works necessary for the construction, maintenance and operation of the canal part of the canal, "and in time of war, as in time of peace, they shall enjoy complete immunity from attack or injury by belligerents, and from acts calculated to impair their usefulness as part of the canal."

But it seems clear that anything, stated or implied, in that Treaty, which is calculated to limit the sovereign rights of the United States in regard to the canal, will be allowed to be forgotten, for the canal has lately, since the question of the control of the Pacific came to the front, shown to the United States even more as a military than as an industrial necessity. In war time the United States will use the canal so that she may mobilise her Fleet in either ocean. Already she has passed estimates amounting to £3,000,000 for installing 14-inch guns, searchlights, and submarine mines at either entrance. She is also establishing a naval base at Cuba to guard the Atlantic entrance, and designs yet another base at the Galapagos Islands. At present those islands belong to Ecuador, and Ecuador objects to parting with them. But it is probable that a way will be found out of that difficulty, for it is clear that a strong United States naval base must be established on the Pacific as well as the Atlantic threshold of the canal. This base, with another at Cuba, would meet the objection I saw raised by an American Admiral last year when he said: "In the event of the United States being at war with a first-class naval Power, I doubt very much whether the canal would be used once hostilities were declared. I assume that our opponent would have so disposed his Fleets as to engage ours in the Atlantic or Pacific coasts according as circumstances might require, and that if we were stupid or careless enough to be caught napping with our vessels scattered, no person in authority with any sense would risk sending our ships through the canal. Our enemy would lie in wait for us and pick off our vessels as they entered or emerged from the canal, and every advantage would be on their side and against us. This, of course, is on the assumption that the opposing force would be at least as powerful as our own. If we had preponderating strength conditions would be different, but if the navies were evenly matched it would be hazardous in the extreme to use the canal. Nor would the fortifications be of much help to us. So long as our ships remained within the waters of the canal zone they would, of course, be under the protection of the guns of the forts, but as soon as they came on the high seas, where they would have to come if they were to be of any use, the fortifications would be of little benefit to them, and little injury to the enemy."

But when to the actual fortification of the canal is added the provision of a strong advanced base near each entrance, this criticism falls to the ground. Between those advanced bases would be "American water," and on either base a portion of the American Fleet could hold an enemy in check until the mobilisation of the whole Fleet.

The world must make up its mind to the fact that the Panama Canal is intended by the United States as a means of securing her dominance in the Pacific, without leaving her Atlantic coast too bare of protection in the event of a great war. Great Britain is the only Power with any shadow of a claim to object, and her claim would be founded on treaties and arrangements which she has either abrogated or allowed to fall into oblivion. Probably it will never be put forward. By a course of negotiation, which, for steadiness of purpose and complete concealment of that purpose until the right time came for disclosure, might be a pattern to the most effective fighting despotism, the American democracy has surmounted all obstacles of diplomacy in Panama just as the obstacles of disease and distance were surmounted. The reluctance of a disorderly sister Republic to grant the territory for the canal was overcome by adding a beneficent one to its numerous useless revolutions. The jealousy of Europe was first soothed and ultimately defied. It is safe to venture the opinion that the reluctance of Ecuador to part with the Galapagos will also be overcome. Then from New York to Pekin will stretch a series of American naval bases—Cuba, Panama, the Galapagos, Hawaii, the Philippines.

The intention, announced on some authority, of the United States to use the canal in times of peace as a tariff weapon for the furthering of American trade may arouse some protest, but it is difficult to see how such a protest can have any effect. The United States will be able to reply that it is her canal, bought with her own money, and that it is her right, therefore, to do with it as she pleases. In a special message to Congress at the end of 1911, Mr Taft urged the necessity for the establishment of preferential rates for American shipping passing through the Panama Canal. He cited the practice of foreign Governments in subsidising their merchant vessels, and declared that an equivalent remission of canal tolls in favour of American commerce could not be held to be discrimination. The message went on: "Mr Taft does not believe that it would be the best policy wholly to remit the tolls for domestic commerce for reasons purely fiscal. He desires to make the canal sufficiently profitable to meet the debt amassed for its construction, and to pay the interest upon it. On the other hand, he wishes to encourage American commerce between the Atlantic and the Pacific, especially in so far as it will insure the effectiveness of the canal as a competitor with the trans-Continental railways." The President concluded, therefore, that some experimentation in tolls would be necessary before rates could be adjusted properly, or the burden which American shipping could equitably bear could be definitely ascertained. He hinted at the desirability of entrusting such experimentation to the executive rather than to the legislative branch of the Government.

In plain language, the United States Government asked for a free hand to shape rates for the use of the Panama Canal so that American shipping interests could be promoted. The shipping affected would not be merely from one American port to another, but between American and foreign countries. By the present shipping laws American "coastal trade" i.e. trade between one American port and another, even if one of the ports be Manila or Honolulu, is closely safeguarded for American bottoms by a rigid system of Protection.

A *Daily Telegraph* correspondent, writing from New York to London at the time of Mr President Taft's message, described the trend of American public opinion which was shown by the changing of the registry of the Red Star liners *Kroonland* and *Finland* from Belgian to American. "This morning Captain Bradshaw, an American, assumed command, and the ceremony of hauling down the foreign flag and hoisting the Stars and Stripes took place. The reasons for the change are not announced, but it is said that the approaching completion of the Panama Canal has something to do with it, and shipping circles here declare that the change of registry presages the entry of the *Kroonland* and her sister ship the *Finland* into the American coast trade between Pacific and Atlantic ports, *via* the Panama Canal. It is expected that a heavy subsidy will be given to American steamships by the United States Government carrying mails from the Atlantic to the Pacific *via* Panama, and it is generally believed that the owners of the *Kroonland* and the *Finland* have this in mind."

Clearly the United States, having expended £70,000,000 directly, and a great deal indirectly, on the Panama Canal, intends to put it to some profitable use, both in war time and in peace time. Naval supremacy in the Pacific in war time, industrial supremacy in peace time—those are the benefits which she expects to derive.

CHAPTER XVI

THE INDUSTRIAL POSITION IN THE PACIFIC

That our civilisation is based on conditions of warring struggle is shown by the fact that even matters of production and industry are discussed in terms of conflict. The "war of tariffs," the "struggle for markets," the "defence of trade," the "protection of our work"—these are every-day current phrases; and the problem of the Pacific as it presents itself to the statesmen of some countries has little concern with navies or armies, but almost exclusively comes as an industrial question: "Will our national interests be affected adversely by the cheap competition of Asiatic labour, either working on its home territory or migrating to our own land, now that the peoples of the Pacific are being drawn into the affairs of the world?"

Viewed in the light of abstract logic, it seems the quaintest of paradoxes that the very act of production of the comforts and necessities of life can be considered, under any circumstances, a hostile one. Viewed in the light of the actual living facts of the day, it is one of the clearest of truths that a nation and a race may be attacked and dragged down through its industries, and that national greatness is lost and won in destructive competition in the workshops of the world. That industry itself may be turned to bad account is another proof that an age, in which there is much talk of peace, is still governed in the main by the ideas of warfare. The other day, to Dr Hall Edwards, known as the X-ray Martyr," a grateful nation gave a pension of £120 a year after he had had his second hand amputated. He had given practically his life ("for you do take my life when you take the means whereby I live") to Humanity. As truly as any martyr who died for a religious idea or a political principle, or for the rescue of another in danger, he had earned the blessing decreed to whomsoever gives up his life for his brother. And he was awarded a pension of £120 a year to comfort the remainder of his maimed existence! At the same time that Dr Hall Edwards was awarded his pension, an engineer thought he had discovered a new principle in ballistics. His bold and daring mind soared above the puny guns by which a man can hardly dare to hope to kill a score of other men at a distance of five miles. He dreamed of an electric catapult which "could fire shells at the rate of thousands per minute from London to Paris, and even further." The invention would have raised the potential homicidal power of man a thousandfold. And the inventor asked—and, without a doubt, if he had proved his weapon to be what he said, would have got—£1,000,000. The invention did not justify at the time the claims made on its behalf. But a new method of destruction which did, could command its million pounds with certainty from almost any civilised government in the world.

In industry also the greatest fortunes await those who can extend their markets by destroying the markets of their rivals, and nations aim at increasing their prosperity by driving other nations out of a home or a neutral market. There is thus a definitely destructive side to the work of production; and some foresee in the future an Asiatic victory over the White Races, not effected directly by force of arms but by destructive industrial competition which would sap away the foundations of White power. How far that danger is real and how far illusory is a matter worthy of examination.

At the outset the theoretical possibility of such a development must be admitted, though the practical danger will be found to be not serious, since it can be met by simple precautions. There are several familiar instances in European history of a nation being defeated first in the industrial or commercial arena, and then, as an inevitable sequel, falling behind in the rivalry of war fleets and armies. In the Pacific there may be seen some facts illustrating the process. The Malay Peninsula, for instance, is becoming rapidly a Chinese instead of a Malay Colony of Great Britain. In the old days the Malays, instinctively hostile to the superior industry and superior trading skill of the Chinese, kept out Chinese immigrants at the point of the kris. With the British overlordship the Chinaman has a fair field, and he peacefully penetrates the peninsula, ousting the original inhabitants. In Fiji, again, Hindoo coolies have been imported by the sugar-planters to take the place of the capricious Fijian worker. Superior industry and superior trading skill tell, and the future fate of Fiji is to be an Indian colony with White overseers, the Fijian race vanishing.

In both these instances, however, the dispossessed race is a coloured one. Could a White Race be ousted from a land in the same way, presuming that the White Race is superior and not inferior? Without doubt, yes, if the coloured race were allowed ingress, for they would instil into the veins of the White community the same subtle poison as would a slave class. The people of every land which comes into close contact with the Asiatic peoples of the West Pacific littoral know this, and in all the White communities of the ocean there is a jealousy and fear of Asiatic colonisation. The British colonies in the Pacific, in particular, are determined not to admit the Asiatic races within their border. That determination was ascribed by a British Colonial Secretary of a past era as due to "an industrial reason and a trade union reason, the determination that a country having been won by the efforts and the struggle of a White Race and rescued from barbarism should not be made the ground of competition by men who had not been engaged in that struggle." But I prefer to think that the reason lies deeper than the fear of cheaper labour. It springs rather from the consciousness that a higher race cannot live side by side with a lower race and preserve its national type. If the labouring classes have always been in the van of anti-Asiatic movements in the White colonies of the Pacific, it is because the labouring classes have come first into contact with the evils of Asiatic colonisation. It is now some years since I first put forward as the real basis of the "White Australia" policy "the instinct against race-mixture which Nature has implanted in man to promote her work of evolution." That view was quoted by Mr Richard Jebb in his valuable *Studies in Colonial Nationalism*, and at once it won some acceptance in Great Britain which before had been inclined to be hostile to the idea of "White Australia." Subsequently in a paper before the Royal Society of Arts Mr Jebb took occasion to say:

"Let me enter a protest against the still popular fallacy that the Pacific attitude (*i.e.* in regard to Asiatic labour) is dictated merely by the selfish insistence of well-organised and rapacious labour. Two circumstances tell decisively against this view. One is that responsible local representatives, not dependent upon labour suffrages, invariably argue for restriction or exclusion on the higher social and political grounds in relation to which the labour question is subsidiary, although essential. The second evidence is the modern adherence to the restriction movement of nearly all Australasians and an increasing number of Canadians, who are not 'in politics' and whose material interests in many cases are opposed to the extravagant demands of labour. Their insight contrasts favourably, I think, with that perverse body of opinion, to be found in all countries, which instinctively opposes some policy of enormous national importance lest the immediate advantage should accrue to persons not thought to deserve the benefit."

But whilst the industrial reason is not the only reason, nor even the chief reason, against Asiatic immigration into a White colony, there is, of course, a special objection on the part of the industrial classes to such immigration. It is for that reason that there has been in all the White settlements of the Pacific a small section, angered by what they considered to be the exorbitant demands of the workers, anxious to enlist the help of Asiatic labour for the quick development of new territories, and in some cases this section has had its way to an extent. Some of the Canadian railways were built with the help of Chinese labour: and Western Canada has that fact chiefly to thank for her coloured race troubles to-day—not so serious as those of the United States with the Negroes, but still not negligible altogether. In Australia it was at one time proposed to introduce Chinese as workers in the pastoral industry: and one monstrous proposal was that Chinese men should be mated with Kanaka women in the South Sea Islands to breed slave labour for sheep stations and farms in Australia.

Fortunately that was frustrated, as were all other plans of Asiatic immigration, and as soon as the Australian colonists had been allowed the right to manage their own affairs they made a first use of their power by passing stringent laws against Asiatic immigrations. A typical Act was that passed in 1888 in New South Wales. By that Act it was provided that no ship should bring Chinese immigrants to a greater number than one for every 300 tons of cargo measurement (thus a ship of 3000 tons could not bring more than ten Chinese): and each Chinaman on landing had to pay a poll tax of £100. Chinese could not claim naturalisation rights and could not engage in gold-mining without permission. Since then the Australian Commonwealth has passed a law which absolutely prohibits coloured immigration, under the subterfuge of an Education Test. New Zealand shares with Australia a policy of rigorous exclusion of Asiatics. In Canada the desire lately evinced of the Western people to exclude Asiatics altogether has been thwarted, so far, by the political predominance of the Eastern states, which have not had a first-hand knowledge of the evils following upon Asiatic immigration, and have vetoed the attempts of British Columbia to bar out the objectionable colonists. But some measures of exclusion have been adopted enforcing landing fees on Chinese; and, by treaty, limiting the number of Japanese permitted to enter. Further rights of exclusion are still sought. In the United States there have been from time to time rigorous rules for the exclusion of Chinese, sometimes effected by statute, sometimes by agreement with China, and at present Chinese immigration is forbidden. The influx of Japanese is also prevented under a treaty with Japan.

The industrial position in the Pacific is thus governed largely by the fact that in all the White settlements on its borders there are more or less complete safeguards against competition by Asiatic labour on the White man's territory: and that the tendency is to make these safeguards more stringent rather than to relax them. Nothing short of a war in the Pacific, giving an Asiatic Power control of its waters, would allow Asiatics to become local competitors in the labour markets of those White settlements.

But debarred from colonisation the Asiatic has still two other chances of competition:

(1) In the home markets of his White rivals in the Pacific;

(2) In such neutral markets as are open to his goods on equal terms with theirs.

The first chance can be swept away almost completely by hostile tariffs, which it is in the power of any of the White nations to impose. There are no Free Trade ideas in the Pacific; the United States, Canada, New Zealand, and Australia, all alike protect their home markets against any destructive

Asiatic competition. If Japanese boots or Chinese steel work began to invade the markets of Australia or America to any serious extent, the case would be met at once by a hostile tariff revision.

The second chance, open to the Asiatic industrial, that of competing with White labour in neutral markets, of cutting into the export trade of his rivals, is greater. But even it is being constantly limited by the tendency to-day which makes for the linking up of various nations into groups for mutual benefit in matters of trade; and which also makes for the gradual absorption of independent markets into the sphere of influence of one or other group. Some students of tariff subjects foresee the day when a nation will rely for export markets on dominions actually under its sway and on a strictly limited entrance to foreign markets paid for by reciprocal concessions. They foresee the whole world divided up into a limited number of "spheres of influence" and no areas left for free competition of traders of rival nations. Under such circumstances a Power would have free and full entry only into those territories actually under its sway. Into other markets its entry would be restricted by local national considerations and also by the interests of the Imperial system having dominion there.

Present facts certainly point to the dwindling of neutral markets. An effort is constantly made by "open-door" agreements to keep new markets from being monopolised by any one Power, and great nations have shown their appreciation of the importance of keeping some markets "open" by intimations of their willingness to fight for the "open door" in some quarter or other of the world. Nevertheless doors continue to be shut and events continue to trend towards an industrial position matching the military position, a world dominated in various spheres by great Powers as jealous for their trading rights as for their territorial rights.

Imagining such a position, the Asiatic industrial influence in the Pacific would depend strictly on the Asiatic military and naval influence. For the present, however, there are many neutral markets, and in these, without a doubt, Asiatic production is beginning to oust European production to some extent. In the textile industries, particularly, Asiatic production, using European machinery, is noticeably cheaper than European. Yet, withal, the cheapness of Asiatic labour is exaggerated a great deal by many economists. It will be found on close examination that whilst the Asiatic wage rate is very low, the efficiency rate is low in almost equal proportion. Some effective comparisons are possible from the actual experience of Asiatic and other coloured labour. In the mining industry, for instance, Chinese labour, the most patient, industrious, tractable and efficient form of Asiatic labour, does not stand comparison with White industry. In Australia Chinese labour has been largely employed in the Northern Territory mines: it has not proved economical.[9] The Broken Hill (silver) and Kalgoorlie (gold) mines in the same continent, worked exclusively by highly-paid White labour, show better results as regards economy of working than the Rand (South Africa) gold mines with Kaffir or with Chinese coolie labour.

The Chinaman has a great reputation as an agriculturist, and at vegetable-growing he seems able to hold his own in competition with White labour, for he can follow in that a patient and laborious routine with success. In no other form of agriculture does he compete successfully with the White farmer. In Australia, for example, where the Chinese are still established as market-gardeners, they fail at all other sorts of farming, and it is an accepted fact that a Chinese tiller will ruin orchard land in a very short time if it comes under his control.

In navvying work and in dock-labouring work the Asiatic coolie is not really economical. To see four coolies struggling to carry one frozen carcase of mutton off a steamer at Durban, with a fifth coolie to oversee and help the voluble discussion which usually accompanies coolie work; and to contrast the unloading of the same cargo by White labour, with one man one carcase the rule, is to understand why low wages do not always mean low labour costs.

When any particular problem of production has been reduced to a practically mechanical process, when the need of initiative, of thought, of keen attention, has been eliminated, Asiatic work can compete successfully with White work, though the individual Asiatic worker will not, even then, be capable of the same rate of production as the individual White worker. But in most domains of human industry the Asiatic worker, in spite of his very much lower initial cost, cannot compete with the European. Intelligent labour is still the cheapest ultimately in most callings, even though its rate of pay be very much higher. In practical experience it has often been found that a White worker can do more whilst working eight hours a day than whilst working ten hours, on account of the superior quality of his work when he has better opportunities for rest and recreation. The same considerations apply, with greater force, to comparisons between White and "coloured" labour.

A fact of importance in the discussion of this point is the effect of impatient White labour in encouraging, of patient Asiatic labour in discouraging, the invention and use of machinery. The White worker is always seeking to simplify his tasks, to find a less onerous way. (He discovers, for instance, that the wheel-barrow saves porterage.) Now that coloured labour is being banished from cotton-fields and sugar-brakes, we hear talk of machines which will pick cotton and trash cane-fields.

The industrial position in the Pacific as regards White and "coloured" labour is then to-day this: Owing to the efforts, sometimes expressed in terms of legal enactment, sometimes of riot and disorder,[10] of the British race colonists in the Pacific, the settlements of Australia and New Zealand have been kept almost entirely free from Asiatic colonists: and the Pacific slopes of the United States and Canada have been but little subjected to the racial taint. Asiatic rivalry in the industrial sphere must therefore be directed from Asiatic territory. The goods, not the labour, must be exported; and the goods can be met with hostile tariffs just as the labour is met with

Exclusion Acts. In neutral markets the products of Asiatic labour can compete with some success with the products of the labour of the White communities, but not with that overwhelming success which an examination of comparative wage rates would suggest. Under "open door" conditions Asiatic peoples could kill many White industries in the Pacific; but "open door" conditions could only be enforced by a successful war. Such a war, of course, would be followed by the sweeping away of immigration restrictions as well as goods restrictions.

There is another, the Asiatic, side to the question. Without a doubt the Asiatic territories in the Pacific will not continue to offer rich prizes for European Powers seeking trade advantages through setting up "spheres of influence." Since Japan won recognition as a nation she has framed her tariffs to suit herself. In the earlier stages of her industrial progress she imported articles, learned to copy them, and then imposed a prohibitive tariff on their importation. Various kinds of machinery were next copied and their importation stopped. China may be expected to follow the same plan. Europe and America may not expect to make profits out of exploiting her development. A frank recognition of this fact would conduce to peace in the Pacific. If it can be agreed that neither as regards her territory nor her markets is China to be served up as the prize of successful dominance of the Pacific, one of the great promptings to warfare there would disappear. "Asia for the Asiatics" is a just policy, and would probably prove a wise one.

In discussing the position of Asiatic labour in the Pacific I have taken a view which will dissatisfy some alarmists who cite the fact that the wage rate for labour in Western Canada and Australia is about 8s. a day, and in China and Japan about 1s. a day; and conclude therefore that the Asiatic power in the industrial field is overwhelming. But an examination of actual working results rather than theoretical conclusions from a limited range of facts will very much modify that conclusion. Asiatic labour competition, if allowed liberty of access for the worker as well as his work, would undoubtedly drag down the White communities of the Pacific. But when the competition is confined to the work, and the workman is kept at a distance, it is not at all as serious a matter as some have held, and can always be easily met with tariff legislation. The most serious blow to European and American industrialism that Asia could inflict would be an extension of the Japanese protective system to the Asiatic mainland. Yet that we could not grumble at; and it would have a compensating advantage in taking away the temptation to conflict which the rich prize of a suzerainty over the Chinese market now dangles before the industrial world.

There are now one or two industrial facts of less importance to which attention may be drawn. The United States, with the completion of the Panama Canal, will be the greatest industrial Power of the Pacific. Her manufacturing interests are grouped nearer to the east than the west coast—partly because of the position of her coalfields,—and the fact has hitherto stood in the way of her seaport trade to the Pacific. With the opening of the canal her eastern ports will find the route to the Pacific reduced greatly, and they will come into closer touch with the western side of South America, with Asia, and with the British communities in the South Pacific. The perfect organisation of the industrial machinery of the United States will give her a position of superiority analogous to that which Great Britain had in the Atlantic at the dawn of the era of steam and steel.

Western Canada is a possible great industrial factor of the future when she learns to utilise the tremendous water power of the Selkirks and Rockies. The Canadian people have the ambition to become manufacturers, and already they satisfy the home demand for many lines of manufactured goods, and have established an export trade in manufactures worth about £7,000,000 a year. Australia, too, aspires to be a manufacturing country, and though she has not risen yet to the dignity of being an exporter of manufactures to any considerable extent, the valuation of her production from manufactures (*i.e.* value added in process of manufacture) is some £180,000,000 a year.

To sum up: in neutral markets of the Pacific (*i.e.* markets in which the goods of all nations can compete on even terms) the Asiatic producer (the Japanese and the Indian at present, the Chinese later) will be formidable competitors in some lines, notably textiles. But the United States should be the leading industrial Power. British competition for Pacific markets will come not only from the Mother Country but from the Dominions of Canada, Australia, and New Zealand. Neutral markets will, however, tend to be absorbed in the spheres of influence of rival Powers striving for markets as well as for territory. A position approaching monopoly of the markets of the Pacific could only be reached as the result of a campaign of arms.

CHAPTER XVII

SOME STRATEGICAL CONSIDERATIONS

Soundly considered, any great strategical problem is a matter of:

1. Naval and military strength; rarely exercised separately but usually in combination.

2. Disposition of fortified stations and of bases of supplies.

3. The economic and political conditions of countries concerned.

Such phrases as the "Blue-water School of Strategy" are either misleading, inasmuch as they give an incorrect impression of the ideas of the people described as belonging to such a school, wrongly representing them as considering naval strength, and naval strength alone, in a problem of attack and defence; or else they rightly describe an altogether incorrect conception of strategy. It will be found on examination of any great typical struggle between nations that all three matters I have mentioned have usually entered into the final determination of the issue; that superior military or naval force has often been countered by superior disposition of fortresses, fitting stations, and supply bases: that sometimes clear superiority both in armaments and disposition of armaments has been countered by greater financial and industrial resources and more resolute national character.

On all questions of strategy the Napoleonic wars will provide leading cases, for Napoleon brought to his campaigns the full range of weapons—military, naval, political, economic; and his early victories were won as much by the audaciously new reading he gave to the politics of war as to his skill in military strategy and in tactics. It would be a fascinating task to imagine a Napoleon setting his mind to a consideration of the strategy of the Pacific with all its vast problems. But since to give to "strategy" its properly wide definition would be to deal again in this chapter with many matters already fully discussed, I propose to touch upon it here in a much narrower sense, and suggest certain of the more immediate strategical problems, particularly in regard to the disposition of fortified stations and bases of supplies.

A glance at the map will show that the British Empire has at the present moment an enormous strategical superiority over any other Power in the Pacific. That Empire is established on both flanks, in positions with strong and safe harbours for fleets, and with great tracts of fertile country for recruiting local military forces and providing garrisons. (For the time being

I put aside political limitations and consider only military and naval possibilities unhampered by any restrictions.) On the eastern flank of the Pacific Ocean is the Columbian province of Canada provided with several fine harbours and allowing of the construction of an ideal naval base behind the shelter of Vancouver Island. The coastal waters and the coastal rivers alike make possible great fisheries, and consequently are good nurseries for seamen. The coastal territory has supplies of coal, of timber, of oil. The hinterland is rich pastoral, agricultural, and mineral country capable of carrying an enormous population and, therefore, of providing a great army.

Considered in relation to its neighbours in the Pacific, Canada is strategically quite safe except as regards attack from one quarter—the United States. A Russian attack upon Canada, for instance, would be strategically hopeless (I presume some equality of force), since a Russian Fleet would have to cross the Pacific and meet the Canadian Fleet where the Canadians chose, or else batter a fortified coast with the Canadian Fleet sheltering in some port on a flank waiting a chance to attack. The same remark applies to an attack from Japan, from China, or from a South American nation. As regards an attack from the United States, the position, of course, is different. But even in that case the strategical position of Canada would be at least not inferior to that of the enemy (apart from superiority of numbers), since that enemy would be liable to diverting attacks from Great Britain in the Atlantic and from Australia and New Zealand in the Pacific (whose forces would, however, have to subdue the Philippines and the Hawaiian Islands before they could safely approach the North American coast). An attack by the United States on Canada is, however, not within the bounds of present probability, and need not be discussed.

The very great importance of Canada to the British position in the Pacific cannot, however, be too strongly impressed. Canada holds the right flank of the Pacific Ocean, and that flank rests upon the main British strength concentrated in the Atlantic. With the loss of Canada British mastery in the Pacific would be impossible. To make the strategical position of Western Canada (naturally very strong) secure there is needed—

(a) A British Pacific Fleet strong enough to meet any enemy in the ocean, and so stationed as to be capable of concentrating quickly either at a base near Vancouver on the outbreak of hostilities, or in the rear of any Fleet attacking the coast.

(b) A greater population in Western Canada with an army (not necessarily of Regulars) capable of defending Canadian territory against a landing party.

On the west flank of the Pacific Great Britain is established at Wei-hai-wei, Hong Kong, the Straits Settlements, Borneo, New Guinea, Australia, New Zealand, and various small islands. There are here possibilities of enormous strength and several points of grave danger.

At the outset let us consider the continental position of the British Empire on the west flank of the Pacific. The occupation of India gives to the British Power at once a great position and a great responsibility. Occupation of India, presuming the loyalty of the majority of the native inhabitants—a presumption which seems to become more and more reasonable with the passage of time—gives great material resources and command of a vast population of good fighting men. It is admitted, however, that these native troops require a certain "stiffening" of White troops before taking the field. To provide that stiffening is the greatest single task of the British Regular army. Strategically, the transfer from Great Britain to India of a large number of soldiers to leaven the native forces is not an ideal system. The distance between the source of supply and the field of operations is so great that in peace it is necessary to have a larger force than would be necessary if that distance were reduced, and in war the repairing of wastage would be a matter of some difficulty. Further, the British soldier, coming from a very different climate, suffers a great deal from sickness in India. A more economical and effective system, if that were found to be politically possible, would be to strengthen the White garrison of India in part from Australia and New Zealand and South Africa in case of war.

The defence of India has to be considered in the light of—

(a) An attack from Japan or China based on a Pan-Asiatic movement.

(b) Internal sedition.

(c) An attack from Russia through Persia.

(d) An attack from Germany allied with Turkey by way of the Persian Gulf.

The two former are the more immediate dangers. But on the whole, India is a far greater source of strength than of weakness. She makes the British Empire a great military power on the mainland of Asia, and she can contribute materially to the strength of the Pacific naval forces.

Passing from India we find the British Empire in possession of several very important strategical positions on or near the coast of Asia, Wei-hai-wei and Hong Kong being the advance stations in the north, and Singapore (the favoured meeting-place of the Pacific squadron of the British Navy) being a well-situated central point. A British Pacific Fleet making Singapore its chief base would be in the best position to dominate the western littoral of the ocean. South of Singapore the large settlements (Australia and New Zealand) are friendly. From the north any possible enemy would be best watched, best met, from a Singapore base. That base would be central for aid from India and South Africa; and it would also be the best point of departure for a Pacific Fleet finding it necessary to rendezvous on the American flank of the ocean.

This is a convenient point at which to call attention to one grave strategical weakness of the British Empire position in the Pacific—the lack of a fortified coaling station near to the centre of the ocean. Between Hong Kong and Vancouver there is no fortified coaling station. There are rumours, as I write, of the want being met by the fortification of Fanning Island, at present the landing-place of the Pacific cable between Vancouver and Norfolk Island. Fanning Island is not an ideal station either by position or natural advantages. But it would be better than nothing.

The strategical position of Australia and New Zealand comes next for consideration. Looking to the future, these British Dominions, which can be grouped under the one title, Australasia, will probably form the most important national element in the South Pacific. Considered at present, Australia must be a source of the gravest anxiety strategically, for it has within its vast, and everywhere insufficiently populated, area one great tract, the Northern Territory, which is practically empty, and which contains to-day twice as many Asiatics as Whites. Embracing 335,000,000 acres, the Northern Territory possesses several splendid rivers, in the inland portion a great artesian water supply, and a wide diversity of land and of climate. On the uplands is a warm, dry, exhilarating area, not very rich in soil, but suitable for pastoral occupation, and giving great promise of mineral wealth. On the lowlands, with a climate which is sub-tropical to tropical, but, on account of the wide spread of the gum tree, is practically nowhere dangerously malarial, every agricultural industry is possible, from dairy-farming and maize-growing to the cultivation of coffee, sugar, sago, hemp, and spices. Almost every expert who has explored the Territory has been struck with its possibilities. Mr Dashwood, the former Government resident, considered the "area of land suitable for tropical agriculture enormous." Mr Sydney Kidman, the great cattle breeder, reported on the land about Herbert River as "ideal cattle country." A dozen other authorities acclaim the pastoral possibilities of the uplands. The probability of vast tin, copper and gold deposits is certified to by every geological explorer.

The Northern Territory thus offers a tempting prize for an Asiatic Power seeking new outlets for its population. Yet, with all its advantages the Territory remains empty. It is known that the Government of Great Britain is profoundly anxious for its settlement. It is an open gate through which an Asiatic invader may occupy Australia. It is an empty land which we do not "effectively occupy," and therefore is, according to the theories of international law, open to colonisation by some other Power.

Further, the Northern Territory is specially vulnerable, because an enemy landing there could find horses, oxen, pasturage, timber, some metals, a good soil, plenty of water, any number of easily defensible harbours—in short, all the raw material of war. And to prevent a landing there is nothing. The local White population is nil, practically; the fortifications are nil; the chances of an Australian force ever getting there to dislodge an enemy, nil.

An ingenious Australian romance (*The Commonwealth Crisis*, by C. H. Kirness), recently published, imagines a "colonising invasion" of Australia by Japan. A certain Thomas Burt and his friend, while on a hunting trip in the Northern Territory, observe the landing of bodies of Japanese troops at Junction Bay. They ride to the south-west to bring the news to Port Darwin, the small White settlement in the Territory. For some years preceding Japan had contemplated a secret "peaceful invasion" of the Northern Territory. The project was planned with great care. First a huge military colony was organised at Formosa, and the men trained in agriculture. Later, the men were supplied with wives. Three months were allowed to elapse, and the men were transported secretly to the Northern Territory. Quite 6000 "colonists" had been thus landed before "White Australia" was able to take any action. Japan, when concealment is no longer possible, officially states through its Ambassador in London that, quite without authority from the Mikado, a private colonising organisation had settled a body of Japanese in the Northern Territory. The Mikado regretted this, and was willing that these subjects should disavow their Japanese citizenship and swear devotion to the British Flag. A deputation from the Japanese colony in the Northern Territory then arrives at Port Darwin to offer its allegiance, and to ask that schools should be established in the new settlement.

From that point the story develops to the downfall of "White Australia" so far as all the north of the Continent is concerned. That romance was, though in some of its details fantastic, in its main idea possible. It was one of many efforts in warning. Such warnings seem to be taking effect now, for the Commonwealth Government is moving at last to colonise the Northern Territory, and to build a railway which will bring it into touch with the more populous portions of the Continent. A scientific expedition was sent recently to investigate the conditions of the Territory as regards productiveness and health. The preliminary report of that expedition (presented to the Australian Parliament October 1911) was generally favourable. It enlarged on the great capacity of the Territory for production, and was optimistic about the climatic conditions:

"Bearing in mind that the country was visited at the time of year when the climate was most suitable for Europeans, the general health was remarkably good. The families of the second generation examined showed no signs of physical deterioration. There are none of the tropical diseases, such as malaria and dysentery, endemic in the settlements; and, as long as the necessary hygienic precautions are observed, there is no reason to anticipate their appearance.

"There are, at present, men who have spent from three to four decades in the Territory, and every one of them compares favourably, both as regards physique and energy, with men of similar ages elsewhere.

"The healthiest and strongest are those, both men and women, who take regular open-air exercises both in the relatively cool and in the hot season.

"Life in the back country, provided the ordinary precautions necessary in tropical parts are taken, is decidedly healthy. The summer months are undoubtedly trying, but the winter months, when at night-time the temperature falls below 40 degrees F., afford recuperation from the excessive damp heat of the summer. In addition, the open-air life is in itself a great safeguard against enervation and physical deterioration."

That bears out the views of those who are in the best position to know the Northern Territory of Australia. Clearly, there are no obstacles to its White settlement except such as arise from the apathy and carelessness of the governments concerned. But with the strategical question of populating the Northern Territory is bound up the other idea of populating Australia itself. In 1904, the Government of New South Wales, one of the Australian states, alarmed by the fall of the birth-rate, appointed a Royal Commission to inquire into the cause. One thing made clear by the investigations of the Commission was "that a very large section of the population keeps down the birth-rate so far as it can, and that the limit of birth-suppression is defined by the limit of knowledge on the subject." That was practically the main conclusion in the Commissioners' report. It probably did not need a Commission of Inquiry to tell the social observer of Australia so much. That the decreasing birth-rate in the Commonwealth was not primarily due to any physical degeneracy of the people, had long been the conviction of all who had had the opportunity and the desire to make the most cursory inquiry into the subject. Not lack of capacity, but lack of willingness to undertake parental responsibility, was the cause of the Australian movement towards sterility. Coming to a conclusion as to "why" was thus an easy task in investigating the dwindling birth-rate. It was quite clear that the Australian cradle did not fill, mainly because the Australian parent preferred to have a very small family.

The evil—it is an evil, for there could be no better, no more welcome immigrants to any country than those coming on the wings of the stork—does not affect Australia alone, but is observable in almost every civilised country. It has successfully defied one of the strongest of natural sentiments. Every sane adult is by instinct desirous of being a parent. But instinct seems to weaken with civilisation and its accompanying artificiality of life. If, on an essentially vital point, it is to become so weak as to be ineffective, and is to be replaced by no ethical or other motive working towards the same end, then civilisation will involve extinction. That is the melancholy conclusion which some pessimists even now come to, pointing to the fact that the White races of the earth, as a whole, despite the still prolific Slav and German, show a tendency to dwindle.

Alarm at such a conclusion may yet prove in itself a remedy. Already there is a general agreement that for the community's good it is well that there should be a higher birth-rate, but, so far, the general agreement lacks particular application. With a further recognition of the fate to which artificially-secured sterility points, there may be an acuter alarm, which will convert the individual not only to good belief, but to good practice. What is wanted is a generally accepted conviction that childlessness is either unfortunate or disgraceful, and that anything but a moderately large family is a condition calling for apology. In Australia that is particularly wanted. There are there—in a new country with plenty of room for many millions yet—none of the excuses which can be held to justify "small families" in more thickly populated lands. It is satisfactory to note that since the Birth-rate Commission aroused the public mind on the subject in Australia, there has been a distinct betterment of the birth-rate; and there has been an end to the old objection to immigration. "Empty Australia" is filling up somewhat more rapidly now; but the process is still far too slow, from the point of view of strategical safety.

With Australia, including the Northern Territory, populated and defended, the strategical position of the British Empire on the Asiatic flank of the Pacific Ocean could be organised on a sound basis. An Imperial Fleet, contributed to by the Mother Country, by Australia, New Zealand, South Africa, India, and the Crown Colonies, having a rallying point at Singapore, could hold the Indian Ocean (which is to the Pacific what the Mediterranean is to the Atlantic) as a "British lake," and this powerful naval force would straddle the centre of the western littoral of the ocean, keeping secure the British communities in the south from the Asiatic communities in the north, and ready to respond to a call from Canada. On the western, as on the eastern flank, there is present all the "raw material" for Fleets and armies—great supplies of coal, oil, timber, metals, fecund fishing grounds, and enormous areas of agricultural and pastoral territory.

When the strategical position of the United States in the Pacific comes to be examined, it is found to be for the moment one full of anxiety. The Power which may, five years hence, have undisputed hegemony of the ocean, holds a difficult position there to-day. The map will show that if the United States had had no expansion ideas at all, in the Pacific or elsewhere, national safety demanded that she should stretch out her arm to take in the Hawaiian Islands. This group, if held by an enemy, would be as a sword pointed to the heart of the Pacific States of the Republic: but held by the United States it is a buckler against any enemy from south or west. A foe approaching the United States Pacific coast would inevitably seek to occupy first the Hawaiian Islands and use them as a base: and just as surely would not dare to pass those islands leaving there an American Fleet. With Honolulu Harbour strongly fortified and sheltering a Fleet of any real fighting strength, the Pacific coast of the United States is safe from invasion by sea (invasion by land from Canada hardly needs to be considered; nor from Mexico). At the present time Honolulu is in the process of being fortified rather than is fortified: and a powerful American Fleet awaits the completion of the Panama Canal before it can enter the Pacific without leaving the Atlantic coast of the Republic unduly exposed.

The Philippine Islands, too, are a source of anxiety rather than of strength at present. When the Panama Canal has been completed and Honolulu fortified, and the Philippines mark the terminal point of an American Fleet patrol, their strategical weight will count in the other scale, for they will then give the American Power a strong vedette post in the waters of a possible enemy. Any attack from the Pacific on the United States would in prudence have to be preceded by the reduction of the Philippines, or at least their close investment. Yet the temporary loss of the group would inflict no great disadvantage on the American plan of campaign. Thus the enemy could not afford to leave the Philippines alone, and yet would gain no decisive advantage from the sacrifices necessary to secure them. In the case of a war in which the United States was acting on the offensive against an Asiatic Power, the Philippines would be of great value as an advanced base.

The ultimate strategical position of the United States in the Pacific cannot be forecasted until there is a clearer indication of how far she proposes to carry a policy of overseas expansion. But in the near future it can be seen that she will keep on the high seas one great Fleet, its central rallying point being probably Cuba, with the Galapagos Islands, San Francisco, Honolulu and Manila as the Pacific bases. At present the Galapagos belong to Ecuador, and Ecuador does not seem disposed to "lease" them to the United States. But that difficulty will probably be overcome, since the United States must have an advance guard to protect the Panama Canal on the Pacific as well as on the Atlantic side. Viewed from a purely defensive standpoint, such a strategical position is sound and courageous. If offensive action is contemplated, on the Asiatic mainland for example, a military force far greater than that existing to-day in the United States must be created.

Japan has consolidated a sound strategical position by the annexation of Corea, Russian naval power having ceased to exist in the Pacific. Japan now holds the Sea of Japan as her own Narrow Water. The possibility of a hostile China making a sea attack can be viewed without dread, for naturally and artificially the Japanese naval position is very strong. Holding the Sea of Japan as securely as she does, Japan may also consider that her land frontier on the mainland is more accessible to her bases than to the bases of any possible enemy.

Russia has been harshly criticised for the conception of naval strategy which gave her one Fleet in the Baltic, another in the Black Sea, and a third in the Pacific. But she was forced by her geographical position into a "straggle" policy. It is extremely unlikely that she will now adopt the policy, recommended to her in some quarters, of concentrating naval strength in the Pacific: though, should the *Entente* with Great Britain develop into an actual triple alliance between Great Britain, France and Russia, that concentration is just possible. It would have an important effect on the strategical position in the Pacific: but is too unlikely a contingency to call for any discussion. The same may be said in regard to any possibility of a great development of power in the Pacific by Germany or France.

The interest of the strategical position in the Pacific thus centres in the rivalry, or friendly emulation, between the United States and the British Empire. Without any very clear indications of a conscious purpose, the British Empire has blundered into a strategical position which is rich in possibilities of strength and has but two glaring weaknesses, the absence of a Mid-Pacific fortress and the emptiness of the Northern Territory of Australia. With a very clear idea of what she is about, the United States has prepared for a thoroughly scientific siege of the Pacific, but she has not the same wealth of natural material as has the British Empire.

CHAPTER XVIII

THE RIVALS

The essential superiority of a White Race over a Coloured Race may fairly be accepted as a "first principle" in any discussion of world politics. There are numberless facts to be gathered from 2500 years of history to justify that faith, and there is lacking as yet any great body of evidence to support the other idea, that modern conditions of warfare and of industry at last have so changed the factors in human greatness that mere numbers and imitative faculty can outweigh the superior intellectual capacity and originating genius characteristic of the European peoples. Nevertheless it must be admitted that the conditions, in warfare and in industry, of life to-day as compared with life in past centuries, have increased the value of numbers and of a faculty of blind obedience, and have proportionately decreased the relative value of individual character. An Asiatic army to-day is relatively better fitted to cope with a European army; an Asiatic factory is relatively more efficient.

It is necessary, therefore, to call to aid all the reassuring records of history if one would keep a serene faith that the future of the Pacific, and with it the future of the world, is not destined to be dominated by the Asiatic rather than by the European. Japan with her fertile people and sterile soil has done so much since she discovered that the test imposed on a people by Christian civilisation is based on their powers of destruction, that there is good reason for the alarm expressed by many thinkers (with the German Emperor as their leader) as to "the Yellow Peril." China, too, awaking now after the slumber of centuries and grasping at the full equipment of a modern nation, reinforces that alarm. It is conceivable that White civilisation may be for a while worsted and driven from some of its strongholds by the arms which it has taught the Coloured Races to use. "Asia for the Asiatics," may be a battle-cry raised in the future not without avail. But in time European superiority must again assert itself.

There are many pessimists who foretell the doom of the White Races coming from a sterility self-imposed for the sake of better ease. They see in every advance of comfort a cause of further weakness, and they picture luxury as rapidly corroding the supports of our society. But it is comforting to recall that every age has had the same gloomy critics, and the Golden Age has always been represented in the past by the pessimists of the present. For myself, I am daring enough to think that the White Races of to-day are neither enervated nor decadent: that in physique, in good health and in sense of public duty they are improving rather than deteriorating; and that the Europe of next century will be more happy, more vigorous and more sane than the Europe of to-day. There *was* a time for the joy of pessimists, but it is a past time, that dismal past century when the industrial epoch rushed on man all unawares, when the clattering machine came to sweep away handicrafts, and the new economic idea of human beings as "hands" affected poisonously all social relations. It was as though a cumbrous wain, well-built for its slow and sedate rumbling, had suddenly been hitched to a rushing steam engine. There were disturbances, clatterings, groanings, and creakings. The period of adjustment was a painful one. But it is passing. Meliorism is the justifiable faith of the future.

The future of the Pacific, I hold then, is with the White Races. At the best, the Asiatic can hope to hold his own continent in security. Japan had the chance of securing a temporary dominance after the war with Russia, and at one time was said to have been on the verge of a struggle with the United States, as an assertion of that dominance. But the cloud passed over. With the opening of the Panama Canal, now a matter only of months, the opportunity of Japan will have finally passed. With the gradual re-establishment of British naval power in the ocean, a re-establishment which will come through the agency of Australia, Canada, and New Zealand, if not through the Home Country, and which will be "anti-Asiatic" in purpose, a further veto will be put on any aggressive ambitions on the part of an Asiatic Power. The statesmen of Japan, indeed, seem to recognise that she has had her day of greatest power, and must be content for the future to be tolerated in her present position as one of the "Powers" forming the great council of the foremost nations. But in considering Japan, allowance must always be made for the danger of the people getting out of the hands of the oligarchy which rules them. The Japanese people, fed fat on praise of their own prowess, may one day force a mad course on statesmen asked to choose between civil and foreign war. Such a war would be doomed to failure for financial if for no other reasons. But it might leave a deep stain of blood on the Pacific.

China—a Federal Republic, and rid of the Manchus if present appearances (1912) are not belied—will have no aggressive ambitions for some years to come. She may insist, and rightly insist, on more honourable treatment from foreign nations. But it is not likely that she will set Fleets ranging over the Pacific in search of conquests. By the time that China has come to a warlike mood—if she does ever come—the White Races will be fully equipped for any struggle. The greatest Asiatic peril, so far as warlike forces are concerned, is of a Japanese-Chinese alliance: and the chance of that is slight, for the two peoples are not sympathetic. It will be noted that the very first official paper of the nascent Chinese Republic is a letter of complaint to the Japanese Government.

If it is agreed that the Pacific will fall, as the Mediterranean did, as the Atlantic did, to the rule of the White Man, the next step is to consider, which people? There is, in addition to much evidence, the temptation of race-pride to suggest that of all the European peoples the Anglo-Celtic (controlling the British Empire and the United States) is inherently the best equipped for world dominance. But that is not nearly so sure as is the superiority of the White over the Coloured Races. The Latin peoples—Italians, Portuguese, Spaniards—have in their day won to lofty greatness. The French—in the main Latin, but with a large element of Celtic and some element of Teutonic blood—were supreme in the world for many generations, and are not exhausted to-day. There is not an incident of Anglo-Saxon history; either of fighting against tremendous odds and winning a victory which the stars in their courses seemed to forbid; or of making disaster glorious by a Spartan death; or of pushing out on some frail plank into an unknown sea—which cannot be matched by some incident equally noble from the records of the Latin peoples or the French people. The Teutons are only now making their bid for mastery: the Slavs may have a great future. The future dominance of Europe may be for any one of the European peoples.

But the position in the Pacific can be simplified for the present by the elimination of all the European Powers but two. Spain and Portugal have had their day there, and have passed away. Neither France, Germany, Austria nor Italy can venture any great force from Europe. Nor is any one of them strongly established in the Pacific. Great Britain would be content with the Atlantic but that her overseas Empire gives her duties and advantages in the new ocean. The Pacific possessions of the British Empire were unsought. But they will be held. The other European Power in the Pacific is Russia, which has been checked but not destroyed there. That the supremacy of Europe—at present held, so far as any enterprises beyond its seas are concerned, by Great Britain—may pass to other hands is not impossible; and that would affect, of course, the position in the Pacific. Speculation on that point, however, is outside the scope of this book, which has attempted to deal with the Pacific conditions of the present and immediate future.

On the facts there must be a further elimination of European Powers in the Pacific, since Russia has no naval forces there and no design of creating such forces. There is at present a natural bewilderment in the Russian mind as a consequence of the recent war with Japan. That struggle destroyed her power in Europe as well as in Asia, and the European balance must be restored first. During the next five years—which will be the critical years—

Russia will not count in the Pacific except as the useful ally of some powerful naval nation—either of Japan, the United States or Great Britain.

Great Britain is thus left as the sole European Power capable of independent effort in the Pacific. Clearly the rivalry for the dominance of the ocean lies between her and the United States. To discuss that rivalry is to discuss the real problem of the Pacific. It may be done frankly, I trust, without raising suggestions of unfriendliness. A frank discussion of the problem, carried out on both sides of the Atlantic, would be of the greatest value to civilisation. For the position seems to be that both Powers are preparing to capture the Pacific; that neither Power can hold it against the other; and that a peaceful settlement can only be founded on complete mutual understanding.

It is true that if the United States decides "to play a lone hand," she may win through if all the circumstances are favourable, for she seems destined to control the resources of all America. It is likely that within this decade the United States Flag will fly (either as that of the actually governing or the suzerain Power) over all the territory south of the Canadian border to the southern bank of the Panama Canal. Intervention has been threatened once already in Mexico. With any further disorder it may be carried into effect. The United States cannot afford to allow the chance of a disorderly force marching down to destroy £70,000,000 worth of United States property. Central America has been marked down for a process of peaceful absorption. The treaty with Honduras (a similar one exists with Nicaragua) shows the method of this absorption. It provides:

"The Government of Honduras undertakes to make and negotiate a contract providing for the refunding of its present internal and external debt and the adjustment and settlement of unliquidated claims for the placing of its finances upon a sound and stable basis, and for the future development of the natural and economic resources of that country. The Governments of the United States and Honduras will take due note of all the provisions of the said contract when made, and will consult, in order that all the benefits to Honduras and the security of the loan may at the same time be assured.

"The loan, which shall be made pursuant to the above undertaking, shall be secured upon the customs of Honduras, and the Government of Honduras agrees not to alter the import or export Customs duties, or other charges affecting the entry, exit, or transit of goods, during the existence of the loan under the said contract, without consultation and agreement with the Government of the United States.

"A full and detailed statement of the operations under this contract shall be submitted by the fiscal agent of the loan to the Department of State of the

United States and to the Minister of Finance of the Government of Honduras at the expiration of each twelve months, and at such other times as may be requested by either of the two Governments.

"The Government of Honduras, so long as the loan exists, will appoint from a list of names to be presented to it by the fiscal agent of the loan and approved by the President of the United States of America, a collector-general of Customs, who shall administer the Customs in accordance with the contract securing said loan, and will give this official full protection in the exercise of his functions. The Government of the United States will in turn afford such protection as it may find necessary."

Under the terms of these loan conventions the independence of Honduras and Nicaragua dwindles to nothing. The purpose of the arrangements was stated by Mr President Taft in his message to Congress: "Now that the linking of the oceans by the Isthmian Canal is nearing assured realisation, the conservation of stable conditions in the adjacent countries becomes a still more pressing need, and all that the United States has hitherto done in that direction is amply justified, if there were no other consideration, by the one fact that this country has acquired such vast interest in that quarter as to demand every effort on its part to make solid and durable the tranquillity of the neighbouring countries."

"Solid and durable tranquillity" means in effect United States control. From the control of Central America to that of South America is a big step, but not an impossible one; and the United States already claims some form of suzerainty over the Latin-American peoples there. It insists upon giving them protection against Europe, whether they wish it or not, and under certain circumstances would exercise a right of veto over their foreign policy. The United States also is engaged in promoting through the Pan-American Bureau a policy of American continental unity. This Bureau was the outcome of the Pan-American Conference convened by Mr Blaine in 1890. The general object of the Bureau "is not only to develop friendship, commerce, and trade, but to promote close relations, better acquaintance, and more intimate association along economic, intellectual, educational and social lines, as well as political and material lines, among the American Republics." "The Bureau for commercial purposes," its Director, Mr Barrett, reports, "is in touch in both North and South America, on the one hand with manufacturers, merchants, exporters, and importers, doing all it can to facilitate the exchange and building up of trade among the American nations, and on the other hand with University and College Presidents, professors, and students, writers, newspaper men, scientists, and travellers, providing them with a large variety of information that will increase their interests in the different American nations." The Bureau publishes handbooks and reports on the various countries containing information relating to their commercial development and tariffs.

There will be held this year (1912) at Washington a Pan-American Conference on trade, organised by the Bureau, "to awaken the commercial organisations, representative business men, and the general public of both North and South America to an appreciation of the possibilities of Pan-American commerce, and the necessity of preparing for the opening of the Panama Canal." "The Conference," says the official announcement, "will have a novel feature in that it will consider the exchange of trade—imports as well as exports—and the opportunities not only of the United States to extend the sale of her products in Latin America, but of Latin America to sell her products in the United States, for only upon the basis of reciprocal exchange of trade can a permanent large commerce and lasting good relations be built up between the United States and her twenty sister American Republics. Heretofore all discussions and meetings have considered only the export field, with a corresponding unfortunate effect on public opinion in Latin America, and her attitude towards the efforts of the United States to increase her commerce with that important part of the world. Another special feature will be a careful consideration, from the standpoint of the business interests of all the American countries interested in the Panama Canal, of what should be done to get ready for greater exchange of trade through that waterway, and to gain practical advantages to their commerce from the day it is opened."

The policy of Pan-America may one day come into effect, and the United States Power command the resources of all America except Canada. (That Canada will ever willingly come under her suzerainty seems now little likely.) But from Cape Horn to the Gulf of St Lawrence is an Empire of mighty resources, great enough to sate the ambition of any Power, but yet not forbidding the ambition to make it the base for further conquests.

Yet, withal, the United States cannot rely confidently on an unchecked career of prosperity. She may have her troubles. Indeed, she has her troubles. No American of to-day professes to know a solution of the negro problem. "There are two ways out of the difficulty," said one American grimly; "to kill all the negroes, and to deport all the negroes; and neither is humanly possible." To allow them to be absorbed by intermarriage with the White population is unthinkable, and would, in a generation or two, drag the United States down to the level of a larger Hayti. A settlement of the black question will one day, sooner or later, absorb the American mind for some time to the exclusion of all else. Neither the acquisition of territories with great coloured populations, nor the extension of suzerainty over half-breed countries will do anything to simplify that problem.

There is also a possible social difficulty to be faced by the United States. The present differences between rich and poor are too extreme to be safe. Too many of the rich despise the poor on the ground that to be poor is to be a failure: too many of the poor hate the rich with a wolfish hatred as successful bandits. The quick growth of material prosperity has cloaked over this class feeling. When there were good crumbs for everybody the too-great wealth of the rich was not so obvious. But the time comes when the United States is no longer a Tom Tiddler's ground where everybody can pick up something: and the rivalry between those who have too much and those who have too little begins to show nakedly.

In short, the United States, justified as she is to keep a superb confidence in her own resources, might find a policy of hostile rivalry to the British Power in the Pacific an impossible one to carry through, for it would not be wise statesmanship on her part to presume that her future history will be, at home and abroad, an uninterrupted course of prosperity.

There is no need to presume that hostile rivalry. On the other hand, there is no wisdom in following blindly a policy of drift which may lead to that rivalry. The question of the future of the Pacific narrows down to this: Will two great Powers, sprung from the same race, take advantage of a common tongue to talk out frankly, honestly, their aims and purpose so that they may arrive at a common understanding?

There are some obstacles to such an understanding. The first is American diplomacy, which, whilst truthful to the point of brusqueness, is strangely reluctant to avow its real objects, for the reason, I think, that it often acts without admitting even its own mind into confidence. The boy who makes his way to the unguarded apple orchard does not admit to himself that he is after apples. He professes to like the scenery in that direction. American diplomacy acts in the same way. It would have been impossible, for instance, to have obtained from the American Government ten years ago a confidential declaration, in a friendly way, of the Pacific policy which is now announced. Yet it should have been quite plain to the American mind after the seizure of the Philippines and the fortification of Hawaii, if the American mind would have consented to examine into itself. Now, it is not possible for two great nations to preserve a mutual friendship without a mutual confidence.

Another obstacle to a perfect British-American understanding is that British diplomacy is always at its worst in dealing with the United States. That combination of firmness with politeness which is used in European relations is abandoned for a policy of gush when dealing with America. Claims for a particular consideration founded on relationship are made which are sometimes a little resented, sometimes a little ridiculed. British diplomats do not "keep their dignity" well in negotiating with the United States. They are so obsessed with the feeling that to drift into bad terms with the great English-speaking Republic would be calamitous, that they give a suspicion sometimes of truckling. There would be a better feeling if relationship were not so much insisted upon and reliance were placed instead on a mutual respect for power and on a community of purpose in most quarters of the globe. Meekness does not sit well on the British manner, and often the American's view of "relationship talk" is that it is intended as a prelude to inducing him into a bad bargain.

It should always be the aim of the leaders of American and British public opinion to encourage friendship between the two nations. But it is not wise to be for ever insisting that, because of their blood relationship, a serious quarrel between them is impossible. True, a struggle between Great Britain and the United States would have all the horrors of a civil war, but even civil wars happen; and it is human nature that relatives should sometimes let bickering, not intended at the outset to be serious, drift into open rupture. The sentimental talk founded, as it were, on the idea that the United States and Great Britain are married and must hold together "for better or for worse," is dangerous.

When Pacific questions come up for discussion in the near future, there is likely, however, to be a modification in the old British methods of diplomacy, for the Dominions of Canada, Australia and New Zealand must be allowed to take part in the discussions; and Australia and New Zealand have a certain impatient Imperialism on which I have remarked before. Their attitude in foreign affairs appears as almost truculent to European ideas of diplomacy. Probably Canada will show the same spirit, for it is the spirit of youth in nationhood, with its superb self-confidence still lacking the sobering effects of experience.

It is a mistaken idea, though an idea generally held in some quarters, that the British Dominions in the Pacific are more sympathetic with American than with British ideas. The contrary is the case. Where there are points of difference between the Anglo-Celtic race in Great Britain and in the United States, the British Dominions lean to their Mother Country. Their progressive democracy is better satisfied with the conditions under the shadow of a Throne, which has nothing of tyranny and little of privilege, than with those offering under a Republic whose freedom is tempered a good deal with plutocratic influences. "To be exactly opposite to everything which is known as 'American'—that is the ideal of Australian democracy," said a responsible statesman of the Commonwealth. The statement was put strongly so as to arrest attention; but it contained a germ of truth. In spite of the theoretical Republicanism of a majority of the Australian people, their practical decisions would almost always favour the British rather than the American political system.

The fervid welcome recently given in the Pacific to the Fleet of American battleships which circumnavigated the world, gave rise to some misconceptions. American press correspondents with the Fleet generally formed the idea that Australia in particular was ready to fall into the arms of the United States at the first advance. But that welcome was in part simply the expression of a warm feeling of hospitality for visitors of a kindred race. For the rest, it was an expression of gratitude for the reassurance which the American Fleet gave that a White Race was determined to be a Power in the Pacific. Great Britain had just renewed her treaty with Japan, which had defeated Russia, and this treaty left the Japanese Fleet as the guardian of the British interests in the ocean. To the Australian mind such guardianship was worse than useless. If it were ever a question between accepting the guardianship of the United States—with all its implied obligations—and modifying their anti-Asiatic policy, Australia, Canada and New Zealand would, without a doubt, accept the first alternative. But they would very much prefer that the British Power should be the guardian of their safety, especially a British Power largely supplied and controlled by themselves.

It is towards that development that events now move. It has its danger in that there may be a growing brusqueness in British negotiations in the Pacific. The Dominions of Canada, Australia and New Zealand (I include Canada because all the indications are that she will now fall into line with the other Pacific British nations), paying so much to the piper, will want to call the tune: and whereas British diplomacy with the United States is to-day a shade too deferential, Australasian and Canadian diplomacy possibly will fall into the other error. Experience, of course, will cure the impatience of youth in time. But it is important that at the outset there should be no occasions for bad feeling. A friendly informal conference between Great Britain, the United States, Canada, Australia and New Zealand, ushering in the opening of the Panama Canal, would provide an opportunity for beginning the frank discussion which is needed.

The position in the Pacific confronting such a conference would be this: that friendly co-operation between the United States and Great Britain would give to the Anglo-Saxon race the mastery of the world's greatest ocean, laying for ever the fear of the Yellow Peril, securing for the world that its greatest readjustment of the balance of power shall be effected in peace: but that rivalry between these two kindred nations may cause the gravest evils, and possibly irreparable disasters.

THE END

Milton Keynes UK
Ingram Content Group UK Ltd.
UKHW030625061024
449204UK00004B/321